# Sea

With her fathe
broken legs, a
about to begin—
Megan Garreg
running of thei
was to the sea, where she would sit on the cliff gazing down into the water—and at Abergwent, the drowned village that lay somewhere in its depths.

One day on her deserted beach she discovered a stranger staring moodily into the sea. He seemed mysterious and withdrawn. He said his name was Owen Morgan. He was a geology student but he had been ordered 'six months hard labour without letting two thoughts rub together' and he had that morning been sacked from his job at the nearby pony-trekking centre.

Megan persuaded him to come and help her on the farm, and together they coped with the lambing, the flock, and even some sheep rustlers.

As Owen's trust in Megan began to grow he told her a little about his past, a past that was strangely linked with the drowned village of Abergwent and—unknown to them—the old story was about to be repeated...

Mainly for girls of 12 and over.

# SEA CHANGE

Anne Knowles

A Hippo Book
Scholastic Publications Limited
London

Scholastic Publications Ltd,
161 Fulham Road, London SW3 6SW, England

Scholastic Book Services,
50 West 44th Street, New York 10036 NY, USA

Scholastic Tab Publications Ltd,
123 Newkirk Road, Richmond Hill, Ontario L4C 3G5, Canada

H J Ashton Co. Pty, Ltd,
Box 579, Gosford, New South Wales, Australia

H J Ashton Co. Pty, Ltd,
9–11 Fairfax Avenue, Penrose, Auckland, New Zealand

First published by Blackie & Son Ltd, 1979
Published by Scholastic Publications Ltd, 1980


Typeset by Computacomp (UK) Ltd, Fort William, Scotland
Made and printed in the U.S.A.
Set in Baskerville

# ONE

A seagull hung for a moment in the air-currents at the cliff top, and then swooped down into the evening. In summer the gulls whirled about like so much scattered paper, but the cold had driven most of them inland and March was too soon for thoughts of returning while there was still ploughing to provide them with a feast. It was an odd, calm day, and the sea was so still and blended so perfectly into the pale sky, that where the one ended and the other began was impossible to tell.

In the distance, a big tanker lay on a false horizon of light, so that a smaller ship, farther out to sea, seemed to float in air and not on water at all. What a strange thing to see a ship in the sky. It should be something old and romantic with a high prow and a great head of sail, Megan thought. A squat black collier like that had no business being so flighty.

She watched until the light-trick faded and the black hull in its proper element again, and then turned her eyes to the two beaches that lay below the headland. They reminded her of summer, as the colours of the day had done, and she longed for the warmth and ease of it after the long bitter season. Winter on a hill farm was nobody's joke, even if you loved the life, which she did.

It was a gull's-eye view of the beaches from high up where she stood, and she could see on either side of a tumble of rocks, the almost inaccessible coves with their fringing sand almost covered by the incoming tide. To the left lay the beach where the holiday-makers would come: not many, it was true, because it was a long rough track to the sands from the road that crossed the burrows high over, but a handful would brave their way down, for all that, each fine day of summer, with their picnics and pushchairs, lilos and sand-buckets, stubbing their sandalled toes on the dusty stones of the track, but determined to battle on to that tantalizing beach.

Once there, they would begin the holiday ritual of swimming and sand castles and spreading themselves out to bake in the sun, gleaming with oil, and dark-spectacled against the glare from the sand.

Only the littlest children seemed to have an eye for the real things of the place: the tiny crabs that scuttled along the shoreline, the washed-up shells, the incredible darting life in the rock pools: but they were not allowed to venture far, and none of these transitory summer people had ever found the way to Megan's own beach. This lay the other side of the headland, cut off by the sea even at lowest tide and protected by a great bluff of sprawling rocks. There was a way down, but even Megan tried not to think about it too hard whenever she descended, and she would not risk it now with every foothold slippery from the winter and once-steady stones loosened by frost. She contented herself by imagining how it would look in the summertime. There would be no litter of paper bags and empty cans as there would on the visitors' beach, no crumbling castles and flooding entrenchments; but only calm, flat sand and one set of naked footprints curling down to the water's edge and retracing themselves, where Megan herself would have been down to swim at low tide.

This was another reason for her longing for the return of summer; so that she could enjoy the luxury of a swim. There was always work to be done on the farm, so the odd moments she could snatch in the water were as good as a holiday to her. She did not envy the summer visitors though. Their lives were as different from hers as the bright clusters of chalets and caravans a mile or so up the coastline were from the grey inland village where the hill men gathered, and where her father went in the evenings to drink beer and talk sheep.

Far below and beyond where Megan now stood, the day cooling round her and low cloud shadows stalking her over the grass, lay another village, drowned deep under the sea. John Garreg, Megan's father, said Wales had lost more villages than ever were found in the first place, by the people leaving them or the sand dunes choking them or the towns' people's reservoirs filling the valleys, and that every man in the country knew a handful of such tales. This story was true though, and he knew it in detail, though few people now had even second-hand memories of the time when Abergwent had stood on a green plateau at the edge of the shore, protected from the sea by high banks of grey shingle, with the little shallow Gwent meandering by to merge itself with the salt water.

The people who lived there had kept very much

apart from the villagers of Llanysaf, up on the hill. There was no real hostility about it, but their lives were different. They had cultivated fields, and their cattle wandered across lush grass to cool themselves and drink at the stream, and the cottage gardens flourished. It seemed a soft life compared to the hill and the windy burrows with their sheep grass and wiry bents. So a stiffness grew up between the two communities, and sometimes flashes of anger, like the time Abergwent stole seaweed for the fields from the place that was Llanysaf's by long custom, or when a farmer high up the hill dammed the Gwent for a sheep dip and Abergwent marched up in force to free the stream again.

Because of all this, it put people of both communities about when Evan Morgan from down below went courting up at the village, the house next to the church. He was a determined young man though, and didn't give a hang how they took it. Neither cool welcome nor bad weather would stop him battling his way up the steep track to see Eira Conwy.

On a day of the spring tides, when the weather had been at its worst for days, he happened to glance seaward as he reached her house and saw, far out to sea, a great wave coming, a great freak of roaring water higher than anything he could ever remember. He ran the last few steps and banged on the Conwy's door, begging Eira's father to come with the tower key so that bells could be rung to warn Abergwent, but Conwy thought he'd gone demented and would not be satisfied until he'd seen the wave for himself. Then they ran to the tower, but it was too late, and before the first bell note could sound the wall of water hit the high shingle and brushed it aside as if it were a handful of dust. Then it seemed as if the earth shook, and loosened rocks from the cliff came hurtling down on the village and the little stream ran mad as storms broke everywhere at once.

It rained and blew for days, and once or twice the earth trembled again and the sea boiled like a pot. One or two people from the lower village had been hauled, shivering and wretched, to safety, but the sea took most of them, and the shifting of earth and water wrecked or swallowed the houses and the church.

No one saw Evan again. He had gone down the track in the worst of the storm, cursing into the wind. 'Damn your bells. Let them rot. You've done for us all.'

Now apart from a few scattered stones and the remnant of fields, Abergwent lay in deep water under the long blue shadow of the cliff. The little squat church with its one reedy bell, and the thick-walled houses, lay roofless and tenanted by fish. At lowest tides, people said, you could see it under the water, but mostly it was only the eye of faith that could part its shadows from the shadowy depth round it.

Sometimes Megan would try to imagine the people who had lived and died there, and would embroider from her own imagination this old story from Llanysaf's memory, told to her as often as pure history when she was little and more believable than a good deal she had learned since. Sometimes in the sound of the waves she would imagine she could hear voices. Perhaps at night they came out of the water and walked on the beach, those long-dead people, and talked of how things were in the old days.

Somewhere in the distance a dog barked, and Megan shook herself free of her thoughts and fancies. Mot was after rabbits again, and it would not be the first time if he were to get stuck in a burrow. He was too light-hearted a dog ever to be a real good one with the sheep. The old bitch Glyn should have knocked more sense into him when he was a pup. Still, he was Megan's good friend and companion, and if he liked to chase rabbit now and again—well, he'd grow out of it.

Megan ran towards the sound of the barking, and there was Mot feathering his tail and looking very pleased with himself, but he was not after rabbits. He was crouched close to an old ewe who was bleating pitifully where she stood. Mot had not yet mastered the art of fixing a sheep with his eye: he was too bouncy, and unable to hold still for long himself; but the ewe was not able to move from him. At first, Megan could not see why, but then she noticed the thin wire round the sheep's leg.

Other members of the flock stood at a distance, watching warily, not sure what to do. The old ewe was one of their leaders, and they felt uneasy at her distress. 'I must tell Dad someone's been setting snares again,' said Megan to herself as she walked over to the trapped sheep. She spoke softly to her, and praised Mot for his action. Fortunately the ewe could not have been ensnared long, or the thin strong wire would have pulled in deep and there would have been a nasty wound to treat. Megan freed her and she ran off, calling to her companions.

'Good boy, Mot. Clever, aren't you?' Megan praised him, and rubbed his ears and pulled at his silky ruff hairs till he squirmed with delight.

'Come on you daft thing,' she said, and put the snare in her pocket.

As they walked on towards the in-by fields she began to think again about the bells, and Evan's curse on them. The Garregs were all staunch chapel, but Megan knew the inside of the little church of St Ysaf very well, and its tower where the six bells hung. It is not often you would find such a ring of bells in so small a place, but they had been given and housed hundreds of years since by a rich eccentric old man wanting insurance for his soul in his last years. He had lived in a big house nearby, long ago taken by time and weather, stones from which could be found in a good many barns and walls in the neighbourhood. The names of the bells were Pax, Laude, Gloria, Johannes and Ysaf Sant. The Welshness in the old man could not bear to let Latin have it all its own way. He had set up a good team of ringers to send intricate patterns of sound from the bells clamouring over the surrounding district, and when there was a funeral, Ysaf Sant spoke out alone to tell everyone about it.

Since the day of the great storm when Abergwent sank under the waves, there had been no ringing. When Llanysaf had shaken off that dreadful stillness that often seems to follow a disaster, and had stirred itself and done all it could for the few people who had been rescued, a great crack was discovered in the bell tower of St Ysaf's. Experts were called in and said it must have been caused by the earth tremor that had brought about the rest of the havoc. The crack caused the great beams that supported the bells to shift, and it took months of work to put everything to rights. Then the first day they were ready to ring the bells again, John Edwards who rang Pax, made the first bad error of his expert life when he got caught up by the rope's flying retreat and hauled off his feet by the turning of the bell, wrenching his shoulder badly and giving himself a real fright.

Then Laude was found to be cracked and Johannes rang out of tune, so there was more expense and trouble in taking them down and sending them to the foundry. Then rats got somehow into the tower and nibbled the rope of Ysaf Sant nearly through, so that when he was tolled at a funeral it came snaking down and nearly killed the verger.

All that put right, there was still no end to the trouble and villagers began to make gloomy confidences to each other that it was only to be expected, it stood to reason, didn't it? So nobody was very surprised when traces of brown powdery dust began to appear on the bell tower floor, and an ominous ticking noise could be heard. Woodworm and death-watch beetle had attacked the main beams and for safety the bells would have to come down. Local people refused to help with the dismantling. They felt it would be asking for more trouble: so a firm from the town came and took down the bells and now they lay silent, wrapped in layers of oiled paper and cloth, their iron tongues lagged and dumb.

The church smelt of woodworm killer now, and joiners were replacing the unsound timbers.

'And that'll not be the finish of it either,' the verger said.

Megan could see the tower in the distance as she walked the long slope to the farmhouse. She'd be glad to get home now, as it was growing very cold, the clouds were settling on the hills and there was a wind stirring. It was a funny old place for weather, and you always had to watch out when you were up on the high land, for the sudden mists and driving rain that could make you lose your way a handspan from home.

The house where Megan lived was set in a grove of trees to ward off the wind, and the trees all bowed over in one direction to prove the force of it. The hills rose up behind, rocky and bleak, and she could see the distant figure of her father coming down Long Way with a small group of ewes that grazed there. He would be wanting to look them over and see to their feet. He kept a very close eye on his flock: so much so that some of the other hill men chaffed him and called him Old Nursey. He didn't mind that though, and flock throve on his attention.

Glyn, dedicated and professional, unlike her boisterous son, crouched and wheeled and darted, keeping her charges well bunched and under her eye. The hill sheep were wily, intelligent creatures, not like the heavy-fleeced, thick-legged beasts of the valley. They were agile as goats, but they had not the goat's deliberate sense of mischief, which was just as well. Megan had her own two goats; a Saanen nanny and her female goatling. The kid had been sired by Mr Griffith the Shop's billy-goat, but it might as well have been Old Nick himself for all the trouble she caused. She got into the feed bins and swelled herself almost to bursting with oats; she got into the garden and neatly nipped the heads off the tender young vegetables. She even went as far as the village one day and raided the minister's greenhouse and his wife's washing line. She ate a dozen or so begonias, one shirt, four stiff collars and a woolly vest. Mrs Garreg had threatened her with the stewpot many a time, but Megan knew it would never come to that.

Megan loved her life at the farm, although it meant hard work and long hours. She and her brother David, who was eleven, had always given a hand about the place, but David was none too fond of the sheep and liked best to be away playing or in the shed with his mates crawling about under the old tractor which served as a whole battalion of tanks in their incessant imaginary wars. 'He'll be off as soon as he's of an age to, I can see that,' John Garreg had observed to his pipe as he watched the boy. 'It'll be Megan who takes on the sheep if anyone does.'

Sometimes when things were really bad, and more had been put into the farm in a year than ever came out of it, he would wonder if the sheep men would ever survive, or whether the day would come when the grass on the hills would grow coarse from lack of grazing and whins tangle over the ancient tracks made by generations of sheep. It was the last thing he wanted, but it fretted his mind sometimes.

Because of this he was determined that Megan should go off to Aberystwyth to the College to learn about other kinds of farming, hear other opinions, see new ways. She could see his point of view, but she had begged a year at home with him first, after she had left school, and now she was settling herself to learn all she could from him, knowing his experience to be worth all the theory she would ever learn. He had not taken much persuading. 'You stay here then girl. Gives me more time to look for someone better to give a hand when you've gone,' he teased her.

Now, as he came down the hill slope, he raised his hand to his eyes, recognized her against the last light and waved. She waved in reply, and quickened her step to meet him.

# TWO

Megan was looking out of the window. That afternoon a sudden cold wind had blown up snow, and now all the hillside was white. Lines of a poem she had had to learn at school were tugging at the edges of her mind. Stiff words, she had thought them, and more like a picture of winter than the reality.

*St Agnes' Eve! Ah bitter chill it was*
*The owl for all his feathers was a-cold*
*The hare limped trembling through the frozen grass*
*and silent was the flock in woolly fold*

She wasn't sure when St Agnes' Eve was, or even who St Agnes was: patron saint of sheep, could she be? If so she'd better get busy, Megan thought, irreverently. The weather was as cold outside as ever it was in the poem, but the hill flock was not in woolly fold. It was scattered over the hillside and over the warren, trapped by this sudden and savage snow. Weather often turned treacherous at this time of year, but it had been so springlike for a week or so that they had been less cautious than they might and to add to the troubles, some hikers had pushed down part of the stone wall where Mr Garreg had penned some ewes who might lamb early, and one or two who were injured, so now they too were up on the hill.

The main part of the flock would come to little harm, sheltered in the lee of walls or snug in the drifting whiteness. After all, they had spent the whole winter in weather like this, with only hay to eke out the poor pickings. It was the group from the in-by that worried him and there was no arguing with him when he set out with Glyn, sternly forbidding Megan to come too, though she felt sure he could do with her help.

The light faded and went and he was not back. Then, at nearly nine o'clock, just after David had been packed off unwillingly to bed, he brought most of the missing sheep home. Once he had seen them safely penned though, he was off again for the final two, disappearing into the huge darkness with the torch at his side bobbing like a firefly along the slope towards the warren. It began to snow again.

One or two of the sheep looked really exhausted, and Megan brought them into the house. She and her mother heaved them across to the hearthrug where they lay steaming in the warmth of the fire, their sodden fleeces smelling like badly washed laundry. The old kitchen clock ticked away slowly, the lamplight shining on the gilded sun that beamed across his face. He'd seen it all a good many times before, Megan thought: tired ewes and orphan lambs by the fire, and the winter outside, cold and bleak, or cold and wet, or cold and snowbound, coming to kick back at you when you thought it was spring.

As time went on the clock's ticking took on an insistent almost frantic sound, and Megan found herself breathing in time with it.

She looked round the room. It looked peaceful enough, with the lamplight and the sheep by the fire and the kettle hissing, but she did not feel peaceful inside. It was a bad night the shepherd was caught in, and she knew he would not come back without his sheep. They were his livelihood, so he must find them whatever the weather and whatever the country. Every penny counts, he was always telling her. 'You can stand all the rich shepherds of Wales on a pinhead.' More than the cost to his pocket though, Megan knew that with her father it was the cost to his pride. Every ewe lost, every lamb born dead, was a grief to him.

'Don't be daft girl,' she told herself. 'Don't sit here and fret. You get out and look for him.'

She knew she must call up some neighbours to help in the search, for if he could walk home unaided he would surely have been back long since, and it would be stupid to go alone to risk finding him in such a state that she could not manage him by herself, and then have to waste precious time going to fetch help.

She signalled to Mot, wrapped herself in a cloak and scarf, and taking a torch from the scullery went out of the house, calling out to her mother that she wouldn't be long. Mrs Garreg ran to the door to call her back, but she was determinedly out of earshot by then.

Martin Jones from Lower Cottage and Elwyn Beynon from Plas Glyn came out willingly to join her, bringing torches and a coil of rope, and they set off in whirling snow that blinded and stung their eyes and made them breathless with the force of it. In the light of their torches they watched it come horizontal with the wind off the sea, the newly falling flakes mingling with the fine white mist of snow that the cold air whirled up from the ground.

'Damn this for weather,' Jones said. 'Duw, I hope your Da's found himself somewhere out of this wind. It's enough to take off an Eskimo's whiskers.'

'Don't go on so, Martin boy. Keep your great mouth shut before your tonsils freeze,' Mr Beynon said as he huddled deeper into his coat. 'Keep your breath for walking, see.'

'Walk, is it? I'll walk as far as you any day.'

They kept up their mock argument as they went, to keep Megan cheerful and to hide their own anxiety. It was a bad night all right, and it was more than likely they hadn't seen the worst of it yet.

When they got onto the warren they quartered the ground as best they could by the light of the torches, shouting to each other across the intervening dark, but the wind caught their voices and tossed them away like so much rag and they gave up and searched in silence. Once Megan thought she had found him as something got up from under a bush in front of her, but it was only an old ewe, startled by the light, who blundered off under the weight of her snowed-up fleece, baaing and protesting: she would have to take her chance now, for Megan could only think of her father.

The cold was right through to their bones now, the three of them in the windy, whirling night. The men wanted Megan to go home. 'You look all like an icicle girl. Get on back with you: we'll find your Dad, don't you fret.' She shook her head, scattering the snow that clung to her nose and eyebrows, and huddled closer into her cloak, which had frozen about her so that it slapped across her boots with its icy hem at every step she took. She could not remember what it felt like to be warm.

They crossed the burrows and moved down towards the cliff edge, each silent, swallowing down fear of what might have happened to John Garreg. Then Mot, who was padding like a shadow at Megan's side, barked once, sharply and stopped with ears pricked, listening alertly.

Martin Jones caught the dog in the sweep of his torch and peered out into the blackness that lay beyond its farthest beam.

'What's he seen then?'

'Don't know. Can't see nothing but snow.'

'Can you hear anything?' asked Megan anxiously.

They waited for the wind to take breath for a moment, and in the lull they thought they heard an answering bark and then a shout. 'This way.' Mr Jones cupped his hands and bellowed across to Elwyn Beynon who had cast his search farther across the slope.

Megan's stomach knotted as she heard the distant shout again, coming not so much from the cliff edge as beyond it. They all ran, buffeted by the wind, to the point where the land fell away to the sea and there, crouched on the cliff, marbled with snow and shaking with cold, lay Glyn, her head pressed to the ground, as near as she could get to the giddy edge, her eyes fixed on something they could not see. They yelled in chorus into the blank darkness below. Seconds passed, breathless, and then a faint call answered them.

'Down here,' a voice said.

'Is that you John?' said Mr Beynon into the torch beam that went searching down the cliff.

'No,' said the voice. 'It's Father Christmas fallen off his sleigh and broken his damned leg, that's who.'

Getting him up the cliff was a nightmare, but between them they managed it at last, and John Garreg lay in a heap on the cliff top, white as a sheet, shaking with cold and shock, and swearing no end with the pain in his legs. It seemed he had been after a lame ewe on the cliff path, stumbled in the dark and pitched over the edge to go bumping and crashing down to where an outcrop had caught and held him.

'Stumbled, my eye,' said Elwyn Beynon. 'That's what brought you down boyo: a nasty old snare, see? It's round your boot now, tight as cheesewire. It'll be those Griffith boys, up to no good again.'

'They might have killed you, Dad,' Megan said angrily.

'Come off it, girl. I'm still here, aren't I? You run off now and tell Dr Gethlin I'll need him to patch me up when these two get me home.'

She ran off, unwilling to leave him but knowing him to be in good hands. Mot went bounding beside her and her torchlight vanished into the dark.

Martin Jones had gone up the hill a way to one of the winter hay stores and fetched back one of the hurdles that they used to protect the bales from the weather.

Mr Garreg made a dramatic face when he saw it. 'Great sorrow was there at the Hall that night,' he declared, 'when they brought home the Squire's son stone dead on a h—' His voice trailed off and he passed out cold, his determined courage quenched at last by pain and exhaustion.

'Quick now, let's get him shifted,' said Mr Beynon. 'We'll save the old so-and-so a few nasty minutes.' Deftly they tied his legs together to keep them still, rolled him swiftly onto the hurdle and covered him with all the spare garments they could muster. 'Come on now, Jones boy, best foot forward. Come on Glyn.'

They set off for home over the rough ground, picking their way by torchlight as best they could, but at least the wind was at their backs now and their faces turned away from the sting of the snow.

'It's a fair old step,' Martin Jones panted.

'Aye,' said Elwyn, 'and he's a fair weight, too.'

'Be glad it's not old Griffith from Hafod. He must weigh at least 100 kilos!'

'Old Griffith could lie there and rot, even if it was his neck he'd broken. Nasty old crook, he is.'

'His boys are as bad. Straight as corkscrews, both of 'em. Well here's the gate then Mr Beynon, and blow me if that's not the two sheep young Megan said were missing, there by the fence and waiting to be let in. See, there's the old ewe and the one with the broken tail, both heavy in lamb by the looks of them.'

'Followed us back, I shouldn't wonder. Not so daft are you?'

The two strays, the lame ewe and her companion, shot in through the opened gate, the latter one helped in by the toe of Mr Beynon's boot, to rejoin their sisters with loud bleats of relief. The stretcher party went on up to the house.

Eira Garreg went very white when she saw the men come in. David was leaning over the stairs, blinking in the light like a ruffled owl.

'Is that Dad home?' he called down.

'Yes it is,' said his mother, snappish with worry, 'so get off to bed now before I strap you.'

He knew she never would, but he ambled sleepily away all the same, quite unaware that John Garreg was hurt.

Just then Megan arrived with Dr Gethlin, who put a hand hard on Mrs Garreg's shoulder before he walked over to the makeshift stretcher. As he bent over it, frowning, its occupant stirred and groaned.

'Too soon, John,' Dr Gethlin said. 'You should have stayed where you were. This is going to be nasty.'

Mr Garreg stayed conscious through every unpleasant moment of the doctor's examination.

'Greedy, aren't you,' Gethlin remarked when he had finished. 'One broken leg's not enough for you. You have to go and break both and make more work for a busy man. I'll make you as comfortable as I can now, and I'll phone for an ambulance to take you to hospital as soon as possible.'

'I can't go to hospital, now you know that. There's too much to be done here.'

'Do what you're told,' said the doctor fiercely 'What else am I to do with you? Mend you with sticky tape and glue like an old pot? Say a spell over you for an instant cure? It's two broken legs you have and if they're not attended to you'll be shuffling round on the stumps, so you'll go to hospital like it or not. If you behave yourself they'll let you come home when the plaster's dry. Glad to get rid of you I wouldn't wonder. Then Eira and Megan can keep you in order.'

'It'll be all right, Dad. You'll be back in no

time, and we'll manage here, won't we Mam?'

'I should hope so indeed,' said Mrs Garreg, and she bustled off to the kitchen to make tea for them all while they waited for the ambulance to arrive.

# THREE

In the clear morning light Megan realized all too well what she had taken on, assuring her father so confidently that everything would be all right, and that they'd manage, though manage they would have to. It would be lambing time soon, when they would have been busy enough under normal conditions. Now, with this backlash winter, things would be uncomfortable indeed, for even when the snow had melted—and it was already beginning to drip into thaw—the ground would be sodden and the first new bite of grass checked by the cold. Then there was the sheer physical effort of helping with the lambing, for not all the ewes managed easily, and manipulation was tiring, heavy work. Worst of all was the knowledge that with the best will in the world, one person can only be in one place at one time, and problems could pop up all over the place, like mushrooms. Mrs Garreg would help, of course, and so would young David after school, but neither of them had John Garreg's skill and knowledge. Besides Mrs Garreg would have her husband to look after, and the house and the garden and the hens, as well as her normal task, at lambing time, of caring for any orphan lambs or twins that the ewes could not cope with. As for the neighbours, they would be stretched to the extent of their own strength themselves. They would come and lend a hand willingly, Megan knew, but it would not be fair to ask. Well then, there was nothing to be done but take a deep breath and get on with it.

She took Glyn and Mot out to the in-by fields, where she checked the walls and looked over the sheep who were penned there. They seemed well enough. Then she walked on up the hill, partly to look round, partly to see if the wind might blow an answer her way. Mrs Garreg was busy in the house, and David had gone off to school. A bus came every morning, bursting at the seams with children from far around, shouting and larking their way to the town. Huw Vagg the driver was as deaf as a post when he turned off his hearing aid, which was just as well for him.

The sky seemed huge and rinsed clean of clouds. The light sparkled off the snow. The beauty of it pierced through Megan's shroud of anxiety, the large loneliness of the hillside clearing her head. She was always aware of this landscape, the background of her life, loving it so intensely that sometimes she would stop and put her hands on some part of it, stone or earth or tree, as if to hold it fast to herself. Cruel though it could be, even while it caused so many of her anxieties, it cleansed them from her. The landscape gave perspective to life, her father said: made you remember your place in the scheme of things.

She wished he were walking with her. So did poor Glyn, who cast anxiously about her as if looking for him behind every hump and tussock. She had searched the house for him that morning, and had followed Megan up the hill from obedience rather than enthusiasm for she was one man's dog, and that man was John Garreg.

Mot was happy enough though, bounding along up the slope and shoving his nose into the wet snow, then rolling delightedly and shaking himself in a shower of powdery white.

Megan looked over a group of ewes that always grazed Clump Hill, and then walked along by the Devil's Hat. The huge grey rock glowered at her from the edge of the scar. An old, alien thing it was, the huge grey rock, brought there by some great scouring river of ice in days before memory, and left there as a child will abandon a toy in a dusky garden. Since the earth movements, the year of the drowning, it had teetered precariously on its high perch, though experts declared it safe enough, but Megan hated it, and would never walk directly beneath it.

'There's a horrid old thing you are,' she called up to it. 'There's no telling what you'd do if you could.'

Walking on down the flank of the hill brought her to the cliff edge, and she stood for a moment looking down at the sea. Then she saw that she was not the only one to be watching the waves come in, for down on the beach a hunched and solitary figure was sitting on a wet rock: a very depressed-looking Canute and a very unsuccessful one too, for every now and then a breaker would send water surging round his feet. He must have been very cold, but he did not seem to notice it.

Megan took a good hard look at him from her vantage point on the cliff. She was wary of strangers, but he looked harmless enough and besides she had the dogs with her, so she scrambled down the rock path to the beach to find out more about whoever he was. She called out to him, and the dogs raced ahead, circling him, with hackles up and growling. To Megan's surprise he seemed scarcely to notice them, and continued to gaze out to the horizon with his arms encircling his knees. She called out to the dogs to be quiet though, and walked as near to the rock where the stranger sat as she could manage without wetting her feet.

'What are you doing?' she asked.

After a pause he said, 'Looking at the sea, as you could well have guessed for yourself.' He did not turn his head towards her, but held out his hand to Mot who sniffed it tentatively, decided he liked the smell of it and began to wag. Glyn, less easily won over, lay down at a distance.

'Aren't you cold?' Megan asked.

'I suppose so,' the voice considered. 'I hadn't thought about it.'

'Where have you come from?'

He turned then, and looked hard at her with eyes as cool and grey as the sea they had been watching.

'You seem to want to know a good deal.'

Megan was abashed. 'Oh dear,' she said, 'I'm sorry, but we don't see new faces much around here. I didn't mean to pry. I'll be off now and leave you to yourself. Come on Mot! Come Glyn.'

She made as if to walk away, but the stranger uncurled his stiff cold shape from the rock and splashed through the shallows towards her. He wasn't much more than a boy: hardly older than herself, Megan thought, with dark hair and eyes, and a familiar, local sort of face, though she had never seen it before: Welsh in looks and voice, and an outdoor complexion, but recently acquired and with an underlying fineness and pallor to it.

'Wait,' he said. 'That was rude of me. It seems to be a habit I have when there's a lot on my mind. That's why I came here, to think things out; to see what's to be done.'

'What about?'

'Me, mostly. What I'm to do next. I've been up at Hafod, at the trekking place,' he explained.

'Old Griffith is it? Surely you don't work for him?'

'No, not now. He gave me the sack this morning.'

'You're well rid of him then,' Megan said cheerfully. 'No one in his right mind would work for that old—' she broke off. 'Oh my goodness, I didn't mean—Well anyway, it's not much like trekking weather, now it is?'

'You don't need to tell me about Griffith,' the young man said. 'I came to work for him in the summer, and it wasn't a bad job then. The sons took the treks out mostly and I looked after the ponies. The people who came were a good lot, really, though one or two would have been better off on a bicycle: shrieked for Mam they did if their pony moved out of a walk.'

Megan had seen the strings of ponies go past in the holiday time: pack-trains laden with passengers who were not altogether sure they were enjoying themselves, and brought up at the rear by one of the Griffith boys, riding cowboy-style and cocky as a bantam. They did not give a hoot for ponies or passengers, as long as there was money in it.

'They shouldn't come to places like old Griffith's,' she said. 'There are plenty of good places they could go, where everything's done properly and the ponies don't work so hard.'

'Don't look so accusing at me. Do you think I didn't find out soon enough what kind of place it was? He paid me little enough for the work I did.'

'Why did you stay then.'

He glowered at her, cold and exasperated. 'Because with me there the ponies got at least some sort of attention, and because I didn't want to leave them in the care of that mean devil Griffith. Bad as he was in the summer, it was nothing compared to what he was like when all the visitors had gone home. He grudges his creatures every mouthful they eat. His bins are empty as my hat, and there's scarcely enough hay in his barns for one pony, let alone twenty. I stole some potatoes from the storehouse to boil up for the poorest of them when the weather turned so wicked, but he caught me at it, and threw me out on my ear. God knows how the poor beasts will manage.'

'And what will you do now?' Megan asked.

'I thought perhaps the sea might throw me an answer,' he said gloomily. 'I want to stay here, for it's a good place, but I must find work of some kind.'

'What sort of work can you do?' Megan asked him.

He stared into space again, melancholy and abstracted. Then he looked at her, considering what to say, as if weighing up in his mind how much to tell of himself. 'I used to know a good deal, once; about geology, mostly, rocks and so forth. Then I got ill and they told me to go away and not think about anything at all for a bit. Sentenced me to six months hard labour without letting two thoughts rub together. The only other thing I know about is horses. That's why I was at Hafod.'

'Why did you come to this part of the beach? It's a long way from Hafod.'

'I like it here. The beach below Hafod's all covered in chalets and shut-up fish-and-chip shops. Besides the rocks are interesting here; the way they've been shaped and shaken into the sea. I can't always keep my mind from working, you know.'

'I haven't seen you here before,' Megan said.

'Perhaps I did not choose to be seen.'

She felt dismissed by this remark, and for a while disinclined to say to him what was in her mind. Anyway, she told herself, it was daft to suppose she might have come across the solution to her own problem in this chance-found stranger. Surely she could not expect to discover the answer washed up here on the beach like a genie in a bottle? Nevertheless she took a deep breath and said quickly, 'Do you know anything about sheep?'

He shook his head. 'Not much,' he said. 'Griffith kept telling me sheep farming's on its way out up here.'

'Well, he's wrong there, the gloomy old so-and-so. He's just found it's easier to fleece the tourists, that's all. You wait till you see our flock.'

'Am I going to?'

'Listen,' said Megan. 'I've an idea.' Then she explained to him about her father's accident, and how she might well have to cope with the lambing alone if no help was to be had. When she had finished he thought hard for a while.

'And do you think it will be any great comfort to your father to take on a stranger who's been a little bit off his head, and who hardly knows a sheep from a goat?'

'Will you, or won't you?' Megan asked, challenging him.

'I will, then,' he decided.

'Come on, we'd best go back and tell my father. He'll be home in a day or so. Mam will put you up till then, I'm sure.' Megan set off up the steep path with great determination, hiding even from herself any doubts she might have about whether she had made the right decision. She had set out to find an answer, and she had found one. Her find came scrambling up the path behind her.

'You don't even know my name,' he protested. 'I'm Owen Morgan.'

'And I'm Megan Garreg. How do you do, Owen Morgan.'

They shook hands very formally, and then set off in the direction of the farm with the dogs trotting along at their heels.

As they approached the house, Mrs Garreg came running out, looking very flustered, and clutching a tea-cloth.

'Oh, you'll never guess what Megan,' she said, not registering the stranger's presence at all in her agitation. 'I really do feel vexed. Your father's been on at them so at the hospital that they are sending him back now, and there's nothing ready. I want him back home, the poor man, of course I do, but I never thought it would be so soon. I wanted to put a bed down near the fire for him so as to be company, and so as not to have to be up and down the stairs all the time, but they said he would be two days there at least and now here he is on his way. Give us a hand, there's a love; I feel all here and there like a bird with two nests.'

'Come on now Mam, don't you worry,' said Megan. 'I've brought us some help,.look. This is Owen Morgan. I'll tell you all about him when we're straight. All right?'

'All right then, Megan. Can you carry one end of a bed for me, Owen Morgan?'

'That I can,' Owen said, 'if I'm shown where it is. How d'ye do, Mrs Garreg.'

Megan's mother gave him a sketchy handshake and shooed him into the house, trailing her tea towel. For half an hour or so the three of them worked very hard making a handy and comfortable place for John Garreg's homecoming so that he would not feel useless and alone in the cold upstairs, and while they worked Megan explained to her mother how Owen and she had met on the beach and how she hoped Owen might give a hand with the lambing.

'Help would be a blessing and no mistake,' Mrs Garreg said. 'What with my man laid up for heaven knows how long and fretting no end at not being able to do anything himself. He's not always an easy man with strangers though, and he won't be in the best of tempers after the journey, I don't suppose, so you'd best keep out of his way when he first comes in, young Owen, and let Megan and me get him comfy before she tells him about you. Don't you worry, though, he'll always listen to her in the end.'

So when the ambulance arrived, Owen went out into the back garden while they got John

Garreg settled. Then Megan came to the scullery door and beckoned him in. 'It's as well you weren't there.' She smiled. 'He was as cross as two sticks and swearing like a whole Troop of Horse but he's in his bed now and feeling very sleepy from some stuff they gave him at the hospital. I've told him you're here.'

He slipped quietly in through the door and found Mrs Garreg standing by the sink. 'Don't worry,' she said. 'Go on in. He won't gobble you up. He's a good, kind man when he's himself, but the long ride up these rough roads properly upset him.'

John Garreg was lying in a narrow bed by the fire, with a cage over his broken legs, so that the blankets rose in a great hump over them. He looked out of his element, like a stranded whale. He spoke to Owen at once, not bothering with introductions.

'Megan says she found you on the beach,' he said. 'Washed up from a shipwreck, were you?'

'I probably looked like it,' said Owen.

Mr Garreg glanced at him sharply from under his long eyebrows. 'You're not a drop-out are you?'

'No sir,' said Owen soberly. 'More a throw-out, you might say, since old Griffith showed me the door. I haven't had much knowledge of sheep; I told your daughter that. I can work hard and learn though, if you'll have me. I pick things up pretty quickly.'

John Garreg went on looking at him and said nothing for a while. Then he stuck a great brown arm out towards Owen from under the white sheets and said, 'You're on then boy. You can start now, for your keep and five pound a week.

It's not much, but I can't afford more. You'll find we live well enough here though and you won't go hungry. My wife's not a Welshwoman for nothing.'

Owen took the proffered hand. 'Done!' he said.

# FOUR

'Now you're stopping, you'll need somewhere to sleep,' Mrs Garreg said. 'You'd best show him the cheese-loft, Megan. He'll be comfy there.'

'There's no cheese there now,' Megan explained. 'Even the smell's gone. Grampy used to keep a few cows and Nan used to make cheese, but we don't bother these days.'

The loft was over the old dairy. It was a plain room, its white paint a good many years old, and it had a wooden bed in it, some tea-chests and some racks full of apples. There was a rug on the floor, though, and a huge armchair, its faded cover gaping in places to reveal an even more faded one underneath. The window was small, but it looked out in the direction of the sea.

'Will it do?' Megan asked.

'I'll be fine here,' he said.

'I'll bring up the oil stove if you'll promise to take care. Then you'll be warm. It's a while since anyone's slept here.'

'One thing,' he called to her as she turned away. 'I suppose you haven't a horse at all?'

The mixture of supreme doubt and faint hope in his voice made her smile. He seemed such a solemn person, remote, without being unfriendly, yet even the possibility of a horse about the place animated him.

'You're set on horses, aren't you? Well, we've just the one.' The candles lit up in his face. 'We call her Cariad,' Megan went on. 'It's a daft name, I suppose, for a pony, but she's a nice old thing and she deserves it. She's nothing special, you know. Just an old cob mare we keep for working about the place, and going up onto the tops to see to the sheep. Dad was all for selling her at one time but with the price of petrol we kept her on.'

'Can I see her?'

'There's impatient,' she chided. 'You'll need to get settled in. Though, come to think of it, you've not much to settle, have you? Haven't you got any belongings? Are they still at Hafod?'

'No, I left them in a place I know along the cliff. There's not much: just a few clothes and some books. I'll get them later on: they'll come to no harm where they are.'

'But won't anyone be worried about you?' she asked.

His voice was flat, colourless, as he answered. 'No one will worry about me,' he said.

'All right then. I'll go down and help Mam with the meal and you come when you're ready.'

When she had left the room, Owen Morgan went to the little window, leant on his elbows and gazed far out towards the sea, and two gulls that had flown inland searching for plough swept down and past him keening plaintively. He stretched his hand out to them, but they wheeled away towards the headland, their wings sharply white against the blue sky.

Megan found her mother in the long scullery at the back of the house, starting to make pastry.

'Doctor's just been,' Mrs Garreg said.

'What did he say?' asked Megan.

'Said your father's an old fool, but there's no cure for that and he'll have to wait patiently for his legs to mend. He said to tell you it's a good thing you've found some help to stop Dad fretting so much. I said he hadn't been well, young Owen, I mean. I hope you don't mind, girl, but I thought it best.'

'That's all right, Mam.'

'He said best thing for him is lots of work outside and not too much time to think. Then he said he thought you must have "serendipity". What's that then, girl? Catching is it?'

'Oh dear no, Mam,' laughed Megan. 'It means coming across good things by accident.'

'Well, that's more than your father did,' said Mrs Garreg. 'Come on now. The poor man will be wanting his food.'

After the meal Megan took Owen to see Cariad. She hoped he would not be disappointed. But then, Griffith's ponies were nothing to write home about and he'd spent the whole summer caring for them, and got the sack because of his concern for them.

The pony was in a small walled patch at the side of the in-by, and she raised her head to them as they approached.

'She's beautiful,' said Owen. 'Is she registered?'

'Registered? How do you mean?'

'She's a Welsh Cob, and a good one. She ought to be in the book.'

'In the book? Talk plain can't you? I know she's a cob, and if this isn't Wales I'm a Dutchman, so she's a Welsh Cob, yes, but she's got no papers or anything. She's a working pony, not a racehorse. Her mother worked here before she did, and her mother's mother before that. Grampy bought Nan a cob mare as a wedding present at Chepstow Market, and there's been one here ever since, but no one's ever bothered with papers. Never worried you, has it, Cariad?' The pony snorted softly and began to search for delights in Megan's pocket.

'Who's her sire then?' asked Owen.

'Old Jim Reece's stallion, over in the next valley. Mean old devil he was. Jim Reece I mean. The horse was as soft as butter; big and strong but so gentle anyone could ride him There's a photo of him somewhere up at the house that I can show you. He's dead now though, and so's Jim Reece come to that.'

Then Owen looked the pony over, and led her up and down, and felt her legs and looked at her teeth, all the while talking and crooning to her as if there were only he and she in the field, and Megan a transparent shadow.

'Come back to the world, will you,' Megan said at last, a little exasperated by all this horse-worship. 'I can't see what's so particular about old Cariad, fond of her though I may be.'

'They say that it takes the eyes of a stranger to see beauty in familiar things,' he said, looking at her coolly. 'She's the best of her kind I've ever seen, and you're lucky to have her.'

Megan felt reproved, but somehow she could not resent it. 'Then we'll ride her up to the tops tomorrow,' she said, 'when we bring the ewes down from Long Ridge. Any creature that stays here needs to be of use as well as an ornament.'

Owen was soon to prove his use, for within a few days lambing was in full swing. The ewes, restless at first, up and down, pacing, would collapse to grunt and grind their teeth, until the little blunt forefeet of their lambs appeared and a final effort delivered the slippery parcel. The lambs were curious creatures, far removed from the conventionally pretty white fluffy creatures of the nursery books. These were harsh coated, dirty grey, their catkin tails quivering with energy as they quested for food. The ewes would baa at them, softly imperative, and they would find their shrill little voices in return. The chorus of 'burrh—meeh' was the background music of their lives as Megan and Owen worked among the sheep. It was a mucky, sweating business, but rewarding, for all that. Each birth was a marvel; each first gasping breath of a lamb as the life kindled in it, its outside life as opposed to the dark life of the womb. Sometimes though, this expected miracle did not happen and the lamb was stillborn. Owen found one disconsolate ewe bleating softly and nuzzling at her lamb. She had licked away the caul, but the little creature lay still and cold. He called to Megan, who picked up the lamb and cleared the mucus from its eyes and mouth and towelled it gently to warm it.

'It's no use,' she said briefly. 'I must go back to the split-eared ewe. She's a difficult one to lamb. Watch this one will you Owen and check she's properly cleansed?'

She handed the cold lamb to Owen. It seemed such a waste, after all the waiting and the effort. He hugged the little body to him, tipped back the dangling head and put his mouth to the clammy little muzzle. He blew very gently until he felt the tiny lungs inflate. He wanted the lamb to be alive, even though it was so obviously dead, so he went on doing it, much as one might go on rocking a baby that had long since fallen asleep. Then, like a small explosion in his ear, the lamb sneezed and Owen nearly dropped it in surprise. A slow, pleased smile lit up the usual solemnity of his face, at the wonder of this little miracle. The lamb, invigorated by its first few breaths, was beginning to weave its wet, rubbery head about, searching for something, and its mother, forgotten during the crisis, got to her feet, recognized her own, and began to baa in a deep soft voice. 'Burrh,' she said, bustling anxiously round Owen. He set the little creature down, and after a few tentative steps and wrong directions it found the food source.

Megan came back then and saw the little group. She was amazed and pleased that the lamb was alive, and she looked afresh at Owen who had coaxed it into living.

His manner since they met had been strange, and abstracted; not ill-mannered or even impolite, but as if her were at a distance from everyone, visible, but apart as though behind glass. Only when talking of his beloved horses had he blossomed into reality. Now that same warmth of feeling shone out of him as he watched the lamb suckle, butting the ewe's udder with its head and jerking its ridiculous tail with pleasure as the rich milk went down.

'You'll be a shepherd yet,' Megan said to him. 'It's a ewe-lamb, too, so there's lucky. The split-eared ewe had a ram. Always does, the old fool. Ah well, it's her fourth season, so she'll be drafted anyway.'

They walked round the in-by, inspecting the yield of lambs.

'You've not many twins,' Owen commented.

'And thankful for it,' Megan replied. 'It's all very well for a lowland ewe, but ours couldn't feed twins on this rough pasture. Mam's got enough to do feeding the orphans we get, without having twins to cope with as well. Anyway the milk powder costs goodness knows what now, so the returns wouldn't be worth it. No, one good strong lamb from each ewe is what we always hope for. Mind you, we're not so badly off here as some. Up on the really high sheepwalks you'd be hard to put to see what they do eat. In the Black Mountains you'd think it was the stones themselves the sheep fed on.' Then Megan laughed and went on, 'Perhaps that's why they look like rocks when they lie high on the hillside. You can go squint-eyed sometimes trying to tell one from the other.'

There was no conversation for a while, as they worked. It did not seem to matter. Megan was used to her own company, and Owen not by nature talkative. Then he began to sing an odd, out-of-tune song to himself.

*Up on the mountain*
*High and steep,*
*Are those rocks*
*That look like sheep?*
*Or are those flocks*
*That look like rocks?*

Seemingly pleased with his effort he sang it all over again, though his face was as solemn as usual.

'Where did you get that from?' asked Megan.

'Out of my poor benighted brain,' he replied. 'It will throw up some great work of genius one day, I don't doubt, but until then one must be content with pearls of little value.'

She looked at him hard. She had never in her life met anyone so odd. Then he smiled, and the sun came out. Quite literally, as if the one had some influence over the other, his face and the landscape lit up together. The difference was that the smile was fleeting, but the sunshine seemed determined to stay. Megan was glad of the warmth of it, for it would give the new lambs a good start and, more than snow or wind or bitter cold, she dreaded a wet season for lambing, with the ground dank and the grazing trampled and the streams swollen and treacherous.

'It's a welcome sight, that sun,' she said. 'Makes it look like real spring. Not that I'll trust it,' she added hastily. 'It'll have something up its sleeve yet.' She looked up at the increasingly blue sky, as if daring any lurking grey cloud to turn in its track.

Mr Garreg was equally cautious about the weather when they went in to see him later on, with the tally of the day's lambs.

'You daren't ever feel your luck's in, with sheep,' he said to Owen. 'There's none of this "safely gathered" feeling in a hillman's life. You can't put your lamb-crop in a barn and lock the door so as you can go indoors and put your feet in the fender. Some springs I've felt I've spent the whole season willing lambs to get born alive and to stay alive, and that if I were to stop thinking of them for one moment they'd all die on me. Sheep do that you know: make up their minds to die they do, no matter what.'

Mrs Garreg interrupted then, exasperated. 'Don't you be such an old silly,' she chided. 'You don't keep your sheep by guess and by God, John Garreg. You know more than most and do more than most and if you lose, it's only after a fight and you know it.'

'It doesn't always serve,' said her husband gloomily. 'And now here I am, hobbled like an old ram past his prime and ready for the knife. The Lord knows what you'll do, Megan my girl, if the weather turns again.' But Megan only smiled at him and went to put the kettle on, for she heard David coming in from school.

'Had a good day?' she asked as he kicked off his shoes and slung his satchel into a corner.

'Not bad,' he said. 'Been busy, have you?'

'Fair to middling,' said Megan.

'I'll give you a hand, Saturday,' he called, as he raced upstairs, shedding his coat and scarf.

'Thanks,' she shouted after him, and grinning ruefully she picked up the wreckage his progress had made.

# FIVE

Owen and Megan were riding up Long Way to fetch in the last of the ewes. David was on watch at home, and dared by Megan, on pain of a waled behind, not to go off playing in the tractor shed and forget his duties.

The air was good, and the turf springy under Cariad's unshod hoofs. They sat double until the slope grew steeper and then rode or walked, turn and turn about, enjoying the morning and each other's company. Above them the hill slope curved in a green arc, hiding the real horizon of the high tops that lay beyond, and on this great cushion of green, rabbits were about their occasions, and one lone hare went loppity-lop in front of them for almost a chain's length before it decided to be afraid, and raced away in ground-devouring leaps.

'Looks like a picture book, doesn't it?' Owen said.

'Looks better than it is,' Megan said. 'All that green. But the soil's thin, you'll get nothing really fat on grass like that. Still, it's lovely, I'll grant you, on a day like this.'

Megan was riding, and she saw that Owen stepped softly, consideringly, as he walked alongside, and was smiling to himself. 'Penny for them,' she said.

'I had an uncle once,' he replied, 'came from somewhere about here I think, and he knew more than I'll ever know about land: rocks, I mean, and land shapes and so on. Knew it by love and by instinct, for he had no schooling to speak of. He'd get me to tell him the right names for things, made me think myself a fine young scholar because I knew them. He used to tell me about the old rocks that lie under Wales, and the volcanoes and the shifting and heaving that made the mountains, and he'd tell me that the earth was a dragon asleep, and to walk soft for fear of waking it. I found myself thinking of that just now.'

Megan shivered. 'He was right, your uncle. That's how I feel about that old rock up there.'

The racing hare, on his way to an urgent boxing match, was streaking up the slope to where the turf met the grey stones of the Devil's Hat.

'That rock on the overhang there, do you mean?'

'Yes, that one, perched on the edge like that, as if something were waiting up there to push it down on you.'

'We're both fanciful today,' Owen said. 'But look, the turf's grown halfway up to it, and there's a little sapling with its roots spread half under it. It must have sat there a good long time.'

'Maybe so,' said Megan. 'Come on now, it's your turn to ride. Take Cariad up to the crest of the hill, would you, and look along the slope to a grove of trees. See if you can spy out a small bunch of ewes. Twenty there should be. They like to keep near the grove out of the wind.'

She watched him canter away up the slope. He

rode very well, she could see that. She had never really learned to ride, not like they do at the schools. She had just scrambled on to Cariad when her father first started taking her with him up to the tops, and from then on she had just kept climbing back on every time she rolled off until the knack had come to her.

The sun was warm on her back and she made no effort to hurry. She had learnt long ago that it was daft to arrive anywhere tired out when you had the return journey to make. Anyway, Owen would need time to spot the sheep and as she had told him, they weren't always easy to see, grazing quietly in the wide and rocky landscape of the tops.

He and Cariad stood in view on the skyline, looking out ahead, and after a while he turned and waved to her. Then when he could see he had her attention he pointed away to something out of her line of vision. Then he held up both hands, with the fingers outspread, put them down again, and raised a single hand with the fingers spread out as before. Only fifteen sheep in view. Well, the others would most likely be in the grove among the trees. They were only scraggy, windbent little things, hardly more than bushes in fact, but they meant shelter and an occasional nibble at twigs, and bark, that the sheep appreciated.

Glyn would soon fetch the stragglers out, Megan thought, and as if she read her mind, the collie bitch rolled an eye upwards and aired her tongue, as if asking for orders. 'Wait now,' Megan told her, 'till we get to the top.' Glyn flagged her tail and stayed obediently at heel. 'You miss your old boss-man, don't you,' Megan said. 'Don't think much of me for a substitute, I know. You're a good bitch though.'

She was that. All the right instinct: just the right amount of eye. She stood no nonsense, but she never nipped or hurried without good reason. She was John Garreg's dog before all else, but she would have picked up and set down sheep for Old Nick himself rather than not work.

They caught up with Owen and Megan asked how many sheep he could see now. 'Still only the fifteen,' he said.

Off went Glyn on command to fetch the sheep, streaking low to the ground in a wide arc to gather them up. None came out of the grove and there were no stragglers anywhere on the open ground. Still the tally was fifteen. 'There's odd now,' said Megan, and checked them over. 'The grey-faced ewe is missing, and the one with the broken tail, and three of last year's lambs.'

Owen looked at her with his mouth open. 'How on earth can you know that. Do you have a map in your head of where every sheep grazes?'

'I don't need a map,' she said. 'Creatures of habit, sheep are. They'll graze where they always graze, and where their mothers grazed if we let them. This is their home, much more than the fields by the house. We fetch them in when we need to, but they'll come back to their own heft the moment they can. We ear-mark them in case they should stray, or a strange dog chase them off, but every shepherd knows his own sheep anyway.'

'Oh come on now. That's a lot of old rubbish,' Owen snorted, unbelieving. 'Everyone tells that old story about knowing each sheep by its face, but that can't be true.'

Megan looked fiercely at him and her voice was tart. 'It's not rubbish at all,' she said. 'With some of them it's easy: an odd marking or colour, a crumpled ear, or something like that; but a good shepherd knows the shape of a sheep's face, the note of its bleating, even the way it moves. You'll see. You'll come to it yourself before long.'

He looked at her, sceptically. 'I doubt that,' he said.

'Maybe, maybe not,' Megan retorted, 'but the point is there are five sheep missing. You go on home with these and I'll take Cariad and look for the others.'

Owen looked at the sheep, bunched and waiting, guarded by Glyn. 'Do they know they're to come with me?' he grinned.

'Don't worry,' said Megan. 'Glyn will tell them.'

'Yes'm,' said Owen deferentially touching a non-existent cap.

'Oh yes,' said Megan. 'That's another thing.'

'What is?'

'We must find you an old hat of some sort to work in. You can hardly wear a headscarf like me, and if you don't cover your hair it'll smell like an old sheep's before long.'

Owen pulled a face and she turned Cariad and went trotting off along the slope in search of the missing animals. The landscape could have hidden a hundred sheep without the least difficulty and the rocks and hillocks began to dance under the intensity of her looking. She thought of that parable in the Bible about looking for lost sheep. True enough, any shepherd would do just that, but it occurred to her, rather irreverently, that often it wasn't love behind the search, or kindness, but that each sheep meant good hard cash to its owner, part of his capital, his investment, his hope of some small profit if he was lucky.

Sometimes though, in the worst of winter when they had dug into deep drifts to fetch the creatures out, when the yelping and excited burrowing of the dogs had shown them the place, well, perhaps there was something of the old story in it, a gladness in a life saved, just for its own sake. Then her mind saw again the great bulk of her father's shape in chapel, reading 'He shall feed his flock like a shepherd and he shall gather the lambs with his arm; and carry them in his bosom, and gently lead those that are with young' and she had seen the pride in Mam's eyes. Shepherds might not be the best in the world at attending service, in fact she'd heard that Cotswold sheepmen used to be buried with a tuft of wool in their hands, to show they had good excuse for not having been to church more often, but there were times, she felt, when they understood the Testament better than most.

Well, these sheep of hers were not buried in snow. There had been not so much as a flake of it since the night John Garreg had broken his legs. No, they had probably just strayed off somewhere. It was not usual, but it did happen, and Megan felt irritated. She had better things to do than spend time looking for them. Still, they had to be found.

She searched and searched until she and Cariad grew tired and cold, but she found nothing. Then as she rode away up the slope, the sunlight on the grass showed her something she had not noticed before: a long line of wheel-tracks along the springy grass. Close to, they were invisible, but distance and the slant of light gave them away, much as a photograph from the air will show foundations of old ruins under the turf.

She studied the tracks carefully. What would have made them? A Land Rover most probably, or something like that, so far away from any metalled road, or even cart track. Mr Garreg had no such luxury, which was why Cariad was so useful to him. Who would be driving about up here, and for what purpose?

Her mind ran on: wondering, theorizing, until she checked herself. 'Now don't you go jumping to conclusions, girl,' she told herself firmly. 'Life's not like the telly you know. There's probably no importance in a few old tyre marks.'

In the end though, she had to turn for home with the sheep not found, and she hated having to tell her father. He was angry, but not with her, only with the possibility that someone might have robbed him, though he was reluctant to believe it had happened. 'There's been sheep taken from Mostyn's farm recently, by people who came with a pick-up truck and drove off with them, cool as you please, but by God I never thought they'd try it here. Mostyn's a little man, half afraid of his own rams, but they know me round here, they'd not dare touch my beasts.' His hands clamped angrily on the sheets and he struggled to sit up.

'It looks as though they may have done,' said Owen, quickly. 'Shall you tell the police?'

'Oh wait now,' Mrs Garreg said. 'We don't really know ours have been taken do we? You might have missed them, Megan love. There's plenty of places five sheep could get to, where you might not see them.'

John Garreg sat up again, furious as an old crippled bull, his voice roaring. 'Don't be damned silly, woman. If they'd been there to be found, she'd have found them.'

Megan put her arms round her mother. 'He's right, Mam,' she said.

John Garreg lay back, with the colour gone from his face. There was wetness on his cheeks.

'Now look,' said Megan. 'The pain's made you sweat. You shouldn't get so cross.' She wiped his face so that her mother should not see the tears of frustrated anger on the big man's face that had sprung up to shame him. His hand tightened on her wrist, thanking her without need of words. She knew how he must feel, pinned down to his bed, shut indoors and helpless.

Owen turned to the door. 'I'll telephone the police,' he said. 'That would be best.'

Next day Martin Jones came to ask if they had seen anything of a black Welsh ram of his, and Dr Gethlin, when he came on his rounds, brought news of other stock that was missing.

'It's as well we told the police then,' Owen said. 'If the thieves are still about there's a good chance they'll be caught. It's pretty certain whoever drove that vehicle across the hillside had something to do with it. No one's going to drive up there for the fun of it.'

'Perhaps they could tell from the tyre-marks whose motor it was,' Mrs Garreg suggested, but Megan was doubtful.

'They weren't really tracks, Mam, just marks where the grass was all bent one way. Still, I can show the police where they are if it will help.'

Megan and Owen went out to check the ewes with their new lambs. All was well. Even the old tailless crone had settled down with her foster lamb. It tugged and butted lustily at her, and the dead lamb's fleece, put round it to fool her, was beginning to come untied.

'Shall I fix it on again?' Owen asked.

'No need,' Megan laughed. 'She won't reject him now.'

'It's a wonder the thieves didn't steal some of these,' Owen said, indicating the ewes with their lambs. 'Surely if they grabbed the lambs, the ewes would follow?'

'True enough,' Megan said. 'Though the ewes can be quite fierce, you know, in defence of their lambs, especially with strangers. Besides, there's nearly always someone about, and the dogs are nearby. I would not want to be on the wrong side of Glyn, or even Mot, if they were protecting the flock. No, the danger will come when we let them out on the sheepwalks again and can't always keep our eye on them: when the lambs are well grown and the ewes have lost some of their mother instinct. It does not last long, you know, but it always amazes me how brave the ewes are when their lambs are tiny. They are such timid creatures for most of the time, but you should see a ewe with her head down, drumming her front feet at something threatening her baby. It's not all bluff either. I've seen a strange dog bowled over until it howled by some of these old girls here.'

Owen was very quiet for a while.

'What's the matter?' Megan asked.

'Must be nice,' he said after a long pause, 'for someone to care that much about you.' Megan looked at him, but his face was shut to her. His thoughts were only for himself, and they worked in silence for a while. Then, as if there had been no lapse of time, he said, 'But then, as you say, it doesn't last.'

# SIX

The next day it began to rain. At first it was fine Welsh mist that did little more than cling to the hair, but as the morning wore on, great black clouds stalked in from the sea, and the drizzle turned to a steady downpour.

The fleeces of the ewes became sodden with it, though they were warm enough, for their oily underfleece was weatherproof and thick. The lambs' curly coats were thin as yet though, and wind-blown rain soon chilled them. Megan and Owen penned in the four sheep that might lamb that day, not even giving them the freedom of the in-by field, for even minutes in such weather could kill a newborn in his slimy birth coat. Once dried off, they were tough little creatures, though they looked so delicate, but that first drying-off was critical. A rough towelling by the ewe's warm tongue to get rid of the stickiness and fluff up the fleece, and the lamb was off to a fine start and ready to get to its second essential, food.

By evening, the grass round the field gate was trampled to mud and every ditch gurgled with water and still the rain showed no sign of stopping. When night came it worsened, and Megan did her late rounds in a downpour that took her breath away. When she got back indoors, she found her father awake, listening to the incessant pattering on the windows.

'Don't worry, Dad,' she said. 'I've got them well sheltered.'

'Maybe,' he sighed, 'but what about the ones on the hill? The streams will be like mill-races by the morning. How many lambs will you find drowned? It's the worst enemy yet, and you know it as well as I do. All summer we fried in the drought till we almost forgot what water looked like, and now we're getting more than we want just at the wrong time. God knows why we do it, Megan. We must all be touched in the head.'

'Try not to worry, Dad. It's late. I'll make you some tea, and then you try and get off to sleep.'

'Count sheep, shall I?' he said, bitterly. 'Aye, dead sheep I'll count. Dead lambs.'

'Try and rest,' she told him again. 'Owen will go out in an hour or so and check the ones nearby. They won't dare die if he's around. He won't let them!'

John Garreg made a great effort to smile, swallowing his anxiety as if it were a stone. 'He's a good boy, that,' he said. 'Lives too much inside himself though. I've never known anyone with less to say about themselves. We know no more about him than when he came. I wish we did.'

'Going to hire a Private Eye then, Dad?' Megan laughed.

'Now then, want to make fun of your father?' he said, as he heaved himself up to drink the tea Megan was making for him. 'It's just that he turns away every question about himself like a coulter turning stones. Never rudely mind, I'll give him that, and there's nothing sinister behind that face: just guarded, like. Mind you, when it comes to *asking* questions he's quick enough. He's keen to learn, and it's a good brain he's got, even if he has been overworking it. Get him to talk about old rocks and stones and he's away. I've learnt no end of things, lying here of an evening, with him telling me about earth's old bones, and why we've got the soil we've got here, and the changes it's been through. Always thought of history as something you count in thousands of years, with all the dates of kings and queens and famous battles, but the history he knows, he counts in millions of years. Makes you feel small that does: a real johnny-come-lately in the scheme of things. It seems he's been making quite a study of the rocks and cliffs up by Abergwent, and so I told him the old story about it. Now that did interest him, and he worried out of me every last thing I knew like a terrier getting a rat out of a hole. Mind you, as I told him, it's all what my father told me, and I doubt it's improved in the telling. Still, he went off down to St Ysaf's to look at the bells, and had a bit of a talk with the verger apparently.'

'I know he went there,' Megan said. 'I met him coming out, when I'd been down to the shop for Mam. He said the verger told him they're thinking of raising funds to rehang the bells.'

'There's always talk of that.' Her father laughed. 'And then they argue among themselves and there's gloomy discussion among the old men and a good deal of wagging of heads and then it all gets shelved again.'

'Maybe, one day...?' Megan asked.

'Maybe,' said John Garreg. He drank his tea and stared into the fire. Megan sat with him, warming her feet. For once there were no orphan lambs lying there waiting for their bottles.

'He's doing well with the sheep then, that boy?' Mr Garreg asked.

'He is, too,' Megan said. 'He's a marvel with them: won't give up. Concentrates so hard on what he's doing, it's almost frightening. If that was how he worked at university I'm not surprised he had a breakdown.'

'At Aberystwyth, was he?'

'Yes, he was.' It was Owen, in the doorway. 'Gossiping, are you,' he said, 'and in the middle of the night, too?' Megan glanced up, afraid he might be angry, but his look was quite normal and his tone light. Perhaps he had not overheard much.

'We were just wishing we knew a bit more about you. Just curiosity, you know.'

'Time I was off on my rounds,' Owen said. He took an oilskin cape from the back of the door, shrugged himself into it and put on his boots. Then, taking the torch in one hand, he reached up with the other for the latch. He paused before opening the door and said quietly, 'I wish I knew more about me, too.' Then he went out into the rain and the door shut behind him. Megan and her father looked long at each other, though they made no comment.

All was well in the in-by field, but when Megan and Owen went up onto the hill early in the morning, they found a lamb dead in the stream. They could see where its hoofs had scrabbled, frantic and ineffective, at the slippery bank.

Many of the other lambs looked shivered with cold but those they caught up seemed warm enough underneath. Some had been expertly sheltered behind rocks and walls by the older, wiser ewes, and Megan was glad to see how well they looked.

Then Owen spotted a small, still shape on the hillside, and made towards it. A young ewe stood nearby, baaing softly. Megan recognized her. Her lamb had been weakly at birth, its lungs full of fluid, and Megan had nursed and cosseted it for days before she would let it out to graze. Now it lay cold as earth and hardly breathing. Megan scooped it up and put her ear to its chest. Then she handed it to Owen. The lamb had no strength left. It dangled from his hands with lolling legs and head. He heard the thick, liquid noise in its chest.

'We'll take it home now,' he said. 'Put it by the fire. Perhaps some brandy?' He made as if to put the cold little creature inside his jacket.

'Look again,' said Megan.

He looked again and saw that the lamb was dead.

For days the rain went on, and showed no sign of relenting. The sound of water was everywhere: pattering on the roof, dripping from eaves, sluicing along every drain and gully. In the village, the stream rose up the arches of the bridge until there was barely a hand's breadth of space under them. People began to discuss filling up sandbags in case the water should top the banks, and everywhere the talk was of the weather and the stock that had been lost.

David and his friends were hopeful that the lower land would flood and keep the school bus from its round, but Mr Vagg came prompt to time each day, glowing with tales of breakdown and disaster occurring to all around but never to himself and his faithful vehicle.

On John Garreg's farm, things could have been

worse. Good shepherding kept most of the sheep and lambs out of danger, that and their own wily instinct for survival, but even so there were losses and Owen took these badly. He would retreat into long periods of silence which oppressed and worried Megan. Not that he ever skimped his work: indeed he had scarcely been in dry clothes for days, but would be out again on the hill-side with Glyn alongside. She had taken to him now, and he seemed to be able to bear her company, whatever his mood. Megan, however, often found him brusque and difficult, and had to remind herself to make allowances for the fact that he had been ill. Between his brooding silences and her father's fretful helplessness, her usual patience was stretched taut and thin.

One morning when they were up on the tops, Megan taking her turn on Cariad, and Owen walking alongside, she felt suddenly that if she did not avoid his company for a while she might well fly out at him: tell him to pull himself together: tell him other people had feelings too, that he might possibly consider. She knew that all kinds of things troubled his mind that he had not seen fit to tell her, and this made her feel angry and unreasonable. She could feel the words she would say to him churning indigestibly inside her, but she would not let herself speak them. She would ride on ahead and cool herself in the empty air of the tops, where a drying wind was at last beginning to blow.

Megan stirred Cariad into a canter and went on ahead, without explanation and without looking back though she heard Owen, surprised out of his silence, call out after her to wait, Glyn stayed at his side, but her own Mot ran with her, tongue lolling as the slope grew steeper.

They came over the crest of the hill, and as they did so a strange noise came up to them on the wind. It was the noise of an engine. There, far below, was a Land Rover, taking the lower track that led eventually to the main road, and by the sound of it, despite its four-wheel drive, pretty thoroughly stuck in a bad patch of mud. Further down, where the track grew wider, and partly hidden by a bluff of rocks, was a larger vehicle, probably a cattle truck. From it, whenever the engine noises stopped, she could hear very faintly the sound of bleating.

The anger in Megan made her throat swell up, and without a thought for what she was about to do she set Cariad at a gallop down the slope. No other pony could have done it, but she knew the terrain and she trusted her rider. Avoiding whins and tumbled rocks she came down the hillside like a fury of revenge, as if fired herself by the feelings that burned in Megan. Mot had to go at full stretch to keep up, and he panted as he ran.

Between Megan and the bogged-down vehicle, the land dropped down and then rose slightly again, making a miniature valley down which a swollen stream boiled and tumbled. Cariad would make nothing of it though. She had jumped water twice as wide. The further slope hid the Land Rover from sight as they went down towards the stream but Megan could still hear the frantic revving of its engine and the useless spinning of the tyres as they missed their bite on the soft ground.

Mot was ahead now, as Cariad slowed her pace

to avoid great heaps of loose stone. At the stream's edge, the dog stopped and began to bark calling Megan's attention to something he could see there, and when she drew alongside, she saw at once what it was.

In mid stream, in a deep pool the water had gouged for itself among the rocks, a sheep had keeled over on its side. They often drank from this pool, but normally they could walk there almost dry-footed, and now the water was running high and fast, and the ewe must have missed her step. Her fleece had soaked up water at once and made it quite impossible for her to get up. As it was she had to struggle to keep her head above the surface. On a little island of rocks, her lamb stood bleating, making little frantic leaps in the air, as if that might in some way encourage its mother to rise.

For one brief moment Megan thought of leaving the sheep for Owen to rescue. She knew he would come after her, and he would not be long. It was only the swiftest passing idea though. She could never go off and leave the poor old girl and her baby in such distress. The sheep in the van were at a distance. This one was here and now, and drowning. She waded through the swirling stream, and Mot half swam, half scrambled alongside, keeping his eyes on the ewe as she struggled to keep her nose out of the brawling water.

It was cold work, dragging the ewe to safety against the impatient pull of the stream, but between them they got her to the bank at last, where she stood coughing and sneezing, and dripping like a sponge, and Megan left Mot to guard her in case she should try to get back to the lamb, which Megan set out to fetch from its rocky island.

She waded back with it: it was a big strong wether lamb, and desperate now for its mother. It struggled so much she came near to overbalancing, but at last she set it down on the bank by the ewe, whereupon it at once began butting its mother's side, to find the warm udder under the soggy fleece.

Megan had been so occupied with the rescue that she was not aware of Owen scrambling and sliding down the hillside, until she heard his angry voice quite close.

'What did you go off like that for?'

Avoiding a direct answer, she said, 'Did you see the Land Rover and the truck?'

'Yes, I did,' he said. 'You must have sharp ears to have heard the engine from over the hill. What were you going to do then, girl? Go galloping up and say "please can we have our sheep back"? They aren't playing games you know. It's a crime they're committing. Goodness knows what they might have done if they'd got hold of you. That idiot sheep did you a good turn. Saved you from your own stupidity.'

All her hot anger, and, as she had to admit, sense of high adventure, emptied away from Megan then, and she began to realize what she had nearly let herself in for. Nevertheless they could not stay passively where they were and let the thieves get clean away.

'Look,' said Owen. 'We need identification. We need facts. Then we must go to the police. How can we get nearer without being seen? Any ideas?'

Megan thought carefully. They could not possibly go straight down the slope for there was hardly any cover, but if they followed the stream down its little valley they would come out quite near to the place where the cattle truck stood parked, and where the bluff would hide them from view.

They led Cariad down as far as they dared, and then tied her to a tree with the dogs for company.

'I hope she won't whinny,' Megan said.

'So do I,' said Owen, 'or she'll give us all away.'

They went on as quietly as they could; each rustle of their footsteps sounding loud enough to wake the dead, though in fact the noise of the struggling engine must have drowned out every other sound for the thieves.

Suddenly there was a change in the pattern of that noise, for with some new trick or manoeuvre the Land Rover had gained a hold with one tyre, and then they must have slewed it round to get a purchase with the other for at last, with what sounded like almost human relief, it heaved out of the mud and stood with quietly panting engine.

'We'd better hurry,' whispered Owen.

They arrived at the bluff that concealed them from the cattle truck and Owen flattened himself to the rocky ground.

'You stay here,' he said. 'I'll go and have a look.'

'I'm going too,' Megan insisted.

'Now's no time to be stupid,' he replied. 'One makes less noise than two. Surely you can see that. Anyway there's no time to argue.'

He crept away round the side of the bluff and she waited, anxious and feeling shivery with an odd kind of excitement which was not altogether pleasant. He was a fair time gone and during that time she watched the Land Rover as it approached. There were sheep in the back of that too: she could hear them, although they were hidden by the canvas top. She could also hear, faintly, the sound of voices, and then, louder, the clatter of ramps and gates. They were transferring the sheep to the cattle truck.

Suddenly, Owen was back with her again.

'Help me remember this,' he said. 'Dark blue Bedford T.K. cattle truck with a red pinstripe line. "Timpson and Partners, Livestock, Surrey" overpainted but you can still see. Short wheelbase, green canvas top Land Rover with no spare tyre on rim. I wrote the numbers on my hand. Then I broke my pencil. Typical, isn't it? Something else too. The older Griffith son is in the cattle truck. The driver is thirtyish, tall and dark, in a black donkey jacket. Then there's another man about twenty I think, in jeans and a plaid shirt. Fair hair he's got and a bit of straggly beard. Now let's go to a phone box, quick, before we forget it all.'

They got back to Cariad as fast as they dared, and then looked back as they heard the vehicles move off, noting the direction they were taking.

'Where's the nearest phone?' Owen asked. 'There's a house not far away, look.'

'That's old Mogg,' said Megan. 'Not on the phone, he isn't. Won't have the nasty thing in the house, he says.'

'There's a call box on the Hafod road. Come on. We'd best ride double. Sorry, Cariad my love.'

The pony made light of their weight, and soon they were on the Hafod road with the little red kiosk in sight. Megan felt nervous, dialling 999. Suppose they didn't believe her?

'Police,' she stammered, when the efficient voice replied. It was all so calm and collected when she got through to them, one would think people reported sheep-stealing as a daily matter. They asked for all the information she had and wrote it down at the other end as if it were a shopping list. It was quite deflating, really, after all the excitement she had felt.

However, they assured her that they would look into it at once, and she felt she would have to be satisfied with that. Owen, however, was not prepared to go home quietly and wait. 'Let's go to Griffith's place,' he said. 'See what we can see.'

'Do you think we ought?' Megan felt doubtful, and to be honest, a little nervous. Some of her courage had gone with her anger.

'Go home if you like,' Owen said. 'I'm going.'

Griffith's house at Hafod was a dour-looking place. A once handsome house now surrounded by corrugated-iron sheds and lean-tos that did duty as stables, mostly painted black, but some so rusty that they would no longer tolerate paint of any colour.

There was also a barn, once handsome too, with its arrow-slit windows and great central arch, but its slate roof was in a poor state, patched with a mixture of iron and plastic, and in places there were great gaps in the stonework.

'Fancy paying good money to come to a place like this,' Megan said, when they arrived at the entrance.

'It sounds marvellous in the ads,' Owen grinned.

They looked cautiously about them, but the place was quiet and no one was to be seen. The house seemed to look down at the muddle surrounding it with a kind of vacant disdain. They tied Cariad to a fence-post, out of sight, and went further towards the house. Mot and Glyn trotted ahead into the yard, but no dog came out to challenge them. Megan recalled them sharply by a whispered command.

'I think the place is empty, all right,' Owen said.

They went in, still very wary, poised either to hide or run if the occasion should arise. Still no one appeared, though, and at last Megan was sure that the place was empty. There were no vehicles in the yard or the open sheds, and there were none of the usual signs of activity that you expect in a yard.

Owen had opened the door of a long shed that stretched all down one side of the main court.

'Come over here,' he called.

Megan went across.

'Smell that,' he said.

Megan breathed in the distinctive, oily reek of close-penned sheep. The floor was thick with droppings, but they were all dry.

'How long ago do you think?' Owen asked.

'Four or five days, I'd say,' Megan replied. 'So these can't have been the ones we saw in the truck today.'

'No,' agreed Owen, 'but I think those came from another direction anyway. We went across country to the Hafod road. It would be a very long way round by a route a lorry like that could take. We haven't looked in the other sheds. There might be sheep still waiting for collection. Mind you, I haven't heard any.'

'There might be fresher droppings though.

Sheep taken more recently,' Megan suggested.

'Come on then, Sherlock.' Owen laughed.

Shed after shed was empty. It was obvious the long one was the main holding place for the sheep. Then Owen opened the door of the barn. In it were half a dozen or so ponies. The air was foul. The creatures stood deep in their own muck and there was no trace of fodder or water anywhere. They had made no noise, no whinny of surprise or greeting, which was hardly to be wondered at, the state they were in. Owen looked at them horrified. Then, in a voice so quiet and cold that it made Megan shiver, he said: 'I hope he rots in hell. He's not just out. He's gone for good. Cleared off and left them.'

They searched everywhere, but there were no more ponies to be found. The others would at least be safe enough on the hillside, getting their own living from the grass.

Suddenly, a car drove into the yard and Megan's heart clutched, but it was a police car. They must have taken action with some speed despite their infuriating calmness on the phone. A police sergeant got out and looked hard at them. Owen explained that they were the people who had rung up about the thieves. 'Well, now,' the sergeant said, 'beat me to it, didn't you. Want to catch the Griffith lad red-handed did you, was that it? It's as well you didn't. He's not a pleasant fellow. Can't say much in favour of any of 'em, come to think of it.'

He smiled cheerfully at them, but when he saw the look on Owen's face, and was shown the reason for it, his expression changed and he said, 'You'd best have a look round, boy, and see if you can't find something for 'em to eat. When I've finished here, I'll find someone to take care of them, don't you worry.'

Owen went off on this errand, and Megan answered the policeman's questions as best she could.

'I'll come up and get proper statements from you later,' he said, 'but it's best I know anything that could put me on their track straight away. The Griffiths are only tiddlers in this game, you see. It's a big racket they've got themselves involved with. Looks to me as though they got scared and ran.'

'But we saw the older son today,' Megan said. 'At least, Owen did.'

'I reckon the big boys brought him back for one final fling in this area,' said the sergeant. 'Then they'll drive down to a slaughterman who's not too fussy, and those sheep will all be joints in a couple of days. After all, whoever saw a leg of lamb with an ear-tag or a fleece mark? How do you prove somebody's juicy meal was your father's livelihood? There's plenty of hotels will pay good money for meat, without being too curious about it.'

The sergeant went to his car and relayed to his station all the information he had gathered. 'I'm at Griffith's, Hafod,' he reported. 'Yes, it looks as though we can nail 'em for something at last.' The radio squawked its approval of this. Obviously the Griffiths were not popular with the law.

'You suspected them anyway then?' queried Megan.

'We had wondered. But then all the whispers we'd had seemed to indicate something far bigger than old man Griffith could organize, and we could not come looking round here without good reason, which he was always careful not to give us, the cunning old devil.'

Owen was back, satisfied that the ponies had been properly attended to. He had moved them on to clean straw in the sheds next to the barn and had given them water, slowly at first for they drank greedily and might take harm from too much. Then he forked down hay for them, and stood by each to see that it was capable of eating. He would not be satisfied until the sergeant had radioed the station yet again to get someone to take on the care of the ponies.

'Well, I think I've seen all I need to see here,' the sergeant said. 'Can you two get home all right? I'd offer to take you back in the car, but I've got more work to do.'

'Don't worry,' Megan assured him. 'Our transport's tied up outside waiting for us. Mind you, I've always wanted to ride in a police car. Another time, perhaps.'

'Oh, you're taking up nabbing thieves as a profession, are you?' The sergeant laughed. 'I'd better owe you a ride some time when I'm up this way. Goodbye now, and thanks for your help. Quick action and a keen eye, you both seem to have. We'll be on to those Griffiths soon enough, don't you worry.'

When the car had driven away they went off to find Cariad, who whinnied with impatience as they approached. She felt she had been tied up and left standing in quite enough strange places for one day, and she would be obliged if they would take her back to her paddock without any further delay.

# SEVEN

Eira Garreg was waiting anxiously at the back door for them. 'Your meal's been ready this hour gone,' she said. 'Where have you been all this long time? Nothing wrong, is there?'

'What've you been doing, girl?' her father's voice called out to Megan. 'I thought you'd gone over the cliff too. Come in by here and tell me.'

When they went in he was sitting up in bed and for the first time he had swung his legs out from their cage and had them propped out over the side of the bed, stiff and white in their plaster casings.

'I told him he shouldn't,' Mrs Garreg said. 'Not without Dr Gethlin or the nurse here to say it's all right, but he never would listen to sense.'

'You be careful, Dad,' Megan chided him.

'Oh, never mind that now,' said John Garreg impatiently. 'Tell me what's amiss. Have we lost any more sheep?'

'We aren't sure,' Owen said.

'Not sure!' John Garreg roared, explosively.

'Just you calm yourself,' Megan said. 'We'll tell you what's happened.'

They told the whole story of what they had seen and done that morning, and Megan explained that they could not tell whether it was Garreg sheep in the Land Rover, or animals from old

Mogg's land that marched alongside the stretch just where they had seen the Land Rover.

'I think probably they'd picked up stray bunches here and there, then bundled them into the truck. A handful from each farm wouldn't be missed half as quick as taking a good many from one person's flock,' Owen said.

'Yes, you're right, of course,' John Garreg said. 'Then after you'd seen them drive off you were too busy playing detective to check our sheep that graze there, I suppose.'

'I'm sorry, Dad,' said Megan.

'Oh, come on girl, I'm only pulling your leg. I'd have done just the same. It's as well you went straight away, so Owen could see to those poor creatures at Hafod. Griffith and his boys had better watch it when they come out of jail. We've long memories round here for men who'd leave stock to starve.'

'They'll have to catch 'em first before they can put them in jail,' Owen said grimly, 'but they'll be there a good long time if they do get caught.'

'Well, they've been twisting the law to suit themselves for years,' Mrs Garreg remarked. 'Well known round here they are, but never well liked. I suppose with a bit more help the police could have put them away years ago, but on the whole we like to set our own wrongs right, and not call in the law. Never seems quite friendly, somehow, setting the police on your neighbours, even if you don't like 'em much.'

John Garreg laughed. 'There's proper logic for you,' he said and put a great hand on his wife's shoulder. 'Where's the food then woman?' he asked. 'I'm shrivelled up inside waiting for these two to come home.'

'Well, you'd best hope the meal's not in the same state,' she retorted, and went to look in the oven.

'Your mother doesn't hold it against me, does she, that I suggested telling the police in the first place, when we first knew about the sheep disappearing?' Owen seemed anxious.

'Don't you worry about that,' Megan assured him. 'There's things you can get away with round here, and things you can't. Steal a man's stock, and you steal his livelihood. Dad would never have believed any local man would do such a thing, if there wasn't such solid proof. Anyway, the whole business was organized by strangers, and English strangers more likely than not, too. The law's welcome to do what it likes with them. You ask anyone in Llanysaf. They'll agree with me!'

David was beside himself with excitement and frustration when he came home that afternoon. 'Some people have all the luck,' he grumbled. 'I spend all day stuck in a classroom while you two are off chasing thieves and dialling 999 and having all the fun. I wish I'd been there. I'd have shown 'em. I'd have got Martin Griffith with my karate chop, and slashed their tyres and then I'd have overpowered the others and tied them up, and handed them over to the police. I'd have got a medal, I expect.'

'You'll get no medal from me if you don't get on with your homework,' his mother said.

It was a mild, calm evening; the first of its kind for many a day. There was only a handful of late lambing ewes in the in-by and they showed no immediate sign of giving birth. 'Come for a walk, Megan,' Owen said. It was neither a question, nor a command. She went with him over the warren and she knew for sure where he was heading, striding out over the hillocky turf.

The beach shone like a mirror where the tide had washed it, and the piled grey shingle was sparkling clean up to the high-water mark. The air was so good you would have paid ready money to breathe it, if it weren't there already, free for the taking.

They clambered over rocks until they stood overlooking the deep, sea-filled hollow that the long-past storm and shift of earth had caused to swallow up the lost village of Abergwent. Owen had not said one word on the way, and now as he stared out to sea, he was equally silent. He sat down on a rock, and was so still for so long that he seemed to have turned to stone himself, but Megan would not break in on his thoughts. She felt it might be disastrous, like waking a sleepwalker. Then he said, without any kind of preamble:

'There was a little boarding house on the sea-front down on the south coast, and one night it caught fire. It was an old, timber-framed building, and they weren't so strict about fire regulations in those days. By the time the engines got there they could not get anywhere near the place. A few people got out, but there wasn't a chance for anyone that was trapped. The manager died trying to rescue his wife, and the whole place was gutted. Then, when it was all over, someone found a baby in a clump of shrubs. It must have been thrown from a window in the hope of saving it. That was me. I was about three months old. Original, don't you think, to be found under a bush? So there I was, whoever I was, with all my little history gone up in flames. One of the rescued guests remembered my father's name was Owen Morgan, but no one seemed to miss me, or my parents, so the dear kind State took me to its bosom and brought me up and named me after my father.'

He looked at Megan. He had never before said so many words all at one time to her in the course of any of their conversations, but she made no comment. She just regarded him attentively, and he went on.

'I suppose I was quite happy. It was the only life I'd ever known. The only times I was upset were when I was handed on to another Home when I'd outgrown the one I was in. They don't do that so much these days. It seems to have occurred to them that kids get attached to the place they live in, and don't want to be posted on again like a parcel, whenever it suits the system.'

'Yes, it must be rotten,' Megan agreed.

'Then I met Will Falkland. He was the uncle I told you about. Not really an uncle you see. Just borrowed. I'd just been moved to a Home the other side of Aberystwyth and he was one of the Uncles. Kids who hadn't got relatives to take them out used to get handed over to people who'd offered to be Aunts and Uncles: just at weekends, and special occasions: things like that. You go and have tea with them, or go to a cinema, or something. Will Falkland and his wife had been doing it for years, but she'd just died when I met him. He had two passions. Horses and fossils. He had the best collection of ammonites I've ever seen.

'Well, no one had ever taken much trouble before to find what interested me, so I'd never really found out myself, and to meet someone who cared that much for anything at all was like a blind going up. I don't know if I was really interested to start with, or whether it was just so as to share something, with just one other person instead of a whole bunch, but I listened to everything he told me, and watched everything he showed me, as if it were the last day of the world. I wished I could have lived with him. I think he'd have liked it too, but perhaps they felt he was too old to have charge of a great strapping lad like me all the time, or perhaps it was because there was no woman in the house. We'd have been happy enough. I know that.

'Still, every moment we could we'd spend together, and he taught me to ride, and he taught me about fossils and about the shaping of the earth, and how the great plates of the earth's crust came joined together like a jigsaw, and how everything moves and shifts and changes in such slow motion that we aren't aware of it, until there's a sudden great dramatic outburst, like Surtsey, or Krakatoa. I thought he'd last for ever. I forgot he was old. He was always there you see. Made me stick at school. Made me try for a place at university; and then once I got there I got involved with work and didn't see quite so much of him as I had done before. There'll be plenty of time in the summer, I told myself. I was just coming up to first-year exams when I got a letter from his solicitor to say he was dead.'

'Oh, I am sorry,' Megan said. 'I felt bad enough when Nan died. You must have been wretched.'

'Yes.' Owen sat on a rock, with his knees drawn up, much as he had been sitting when they first met. He was twisting a bit of old sheep's wool between his fingers, and for a while relapsed once more into silence.

Then he went on, in a voice so quiet Megan had to strain to hear him.

'I did not want to believe it. It was a long time before I could. I worked all hours, I drove myself. I couldn't tell you why. Perhaps I thought if I slogged hard enough I'd deserve him not to be dead. It didn't work though. I passed the exams all right, but nothing was changed and I cracked up altogether. The only thing I could think about was the fact that I did not know who I was. It had never worried me before you see. I was no more jealous of kids with parents than I was of the ones with bigger and better bikes, or more pocket money, or whatever. Now I was desperate to find out about myself, and of course I had no better luck than the authorities had had all those years ago.'

'I should think by now there'd be nothing left to find,' Megan said.

'Well,' said Owen, 'I did find one thing. You know I'm a bit off my head already, so I suppose you won't think any the worse of me if I show you. It's the reason I came to Hafod, or to this part of Wales, anyway. I found it in a tatty old bookshop in the back streets of Aberystwyth.'

He took from his pocket a small brown leather-covered book, very old and stained, and with many of the pages standing proud of the binding. It was a book of hymns and poems in Welsh, and on the flyleaf, in ink that was rusted brown, were the words "Owen Morgan, Abergwent".

'I know,' said Owen quickly, as Megan glanced up at him. 'I know the streets of Wales are paved with Owen Morgans. I know it's only a chance that a great- or great-great-grandfather I had was called Owen. But when I opened that book, it was like being hit in the stomach. So I came to look for Abergwent, and found that it wasn't there any more. No village, no existing records. I'm a person who doesn't exist, and if I'm from anywhere it's from a place that doesn't exist. That's not much comfort when you are trying to find yourself. There are those cliffs there, showing me their history in millions of years, but sea and fire between them have wiped mine clean away.'

Megan put a hand on his arm. He looked so lonely and she wanted to comfort him, but she could think of nothing to say. There had certainly been a big family of Morgans in Abergwent, but as Owen had said Morgans were hardly uncommon in Wales.

For a long time they sat and watched the calm cold sea heave and wrinkle like the skin of a beast; a hippopotamus perhaps, or a great grey serpent.

'I like you Megan,' Owen said. 'There may not be much of you, but you fill up all my empty spaces. Can you understand that? You're lucky you see. You and your family are all part of a pattern, while I've always been a useless bit of jigsaw that got lost under the carpet.'

'Well I found you, didn't I?' said Megan. 'Though I don't recall any carpet on the beach.' She laughed, and that made him laugh too. The solemn mood of his revelation vanished, and they ran off across the sand to throw stones into the sea to the great annoyance of the gulls who had hoped for something more edible.

There was a light-heartedness in Owen now,

released from things far better said than kept, and Megan was so delighted that he had broken his silence to her that there seemed good reason to race on the beach and splash through the cold shallows, disturbing the crabs in their antique armour and sending them scuttling to the safety of the rock pools.

It was good to be able to play, to relax for a time, to forget about sheep and the farm and earning a living. There was a while yet before the sun would go down, and the darkness call them back to work again.

When they did go back to the farm by last light, they found John Garreg spreadeagled on a big armchair by the fire. 'Don't ask me how he got there,' his wife grumbled. 'I was putting sheets away upstairs when I heard a noise like someone moving house, and when I came down I found him in his old chair.'

'The pixies carried me,' John Garreg said, his face one enormous triumphant smile.

Eira Garreg grinned back at him. 'I'm thinking those would need to be quite some pixies,' she said, and flicked a duster at him as he lay there, as if he were a wardrobe or an old oak chest.

Just then the telephone rang, and David came clattering down from his room to answer it. He and his friends often chatted at length together on the phone, organizing expeditions and plotting the normal mischief of small boys. This time, though, his conversation was very brief and sounded much too respectful to have been addressed to any of his cronies. Then he came into the room, his face bright with excitement. 'They've got them, Dad. They nabbed them on the motorway. They'd had road blocks out and everything, and that was an Inspector that spoke to me and he says there are three sheep found with our ear-mark, and all the men have been charged. He says Martin Griffith sang like a bird—'

'I bet he never said that,' laughed Megan.

'Well, he said he'd given them the information they wanted, something like that. It's just like the telly, isn't it?'

'It sounds to me as if you've been seeing a deal too much of it,' said his father. ' "Sang like a bird" indeed!'

'Sorry Dad. It's good though, isn't it? Good they've been caught, I mean. And it's all because of Owen and our Megan. Proper pair of heroes, aren't you?'

'Working heroes, I hope,' said John Garreg. 'Have you checked those last ewes, Owen boy?'

'No, Mr Garreg, but I'm just off. I'm glad you'll get some of your sheep back, at least. Have they got old man Griffith and the other boy yet?'

'No,' said David. 'But they know where to look for them. "Just a matter of time" the Inspector said.'

Megan wondered how the story would get told at school in the morning. She suspected it would be 'my friend the Inspector said' and 'as I told the Inspector'. Well, she didn't blame him. Life could be a bit short of adventure for a boy's taste, and David was a glutton for it.

She put on her cloak, picked up her torch from the scullery table, and went out into the dark to help Owen with the sheep.

# EIGHT

Megan was down early in the morning. She liked to talk to her father then to tell him about the day; to ask his advice. It wasn't just that she felt it made him feel useful. She valued his knowledge, and was sure she would never learn all he knew in a hundred years.

'What are you going to get up to today, Dad?' she teased him. 'Doing the Highland Fling?'

'More than likely,' he said.

For a while they discussed the lamb crop and the plans for the coming year: the drafting of some older ewes; when to send on the wethers for fattening in the valleys, what the market price was likely to be. They spoke of dipping and shearing, and whether next season they really would get round to trying Border Leicester rams on the ewes. John Garreg had thought of it for a good many years now.

'A good many people do it. We'd get a heavier lamb, you know,' he said.

'But likely not so hardy,' Megan answered.

'Well, you won't have to worry about it. You'll be too busy with your books by then.'

'Do I have to go, Dad?' she asked. She still felt reluctant to leave the farm.

'No question of that. You've got to be clever enough to keep me and your Ma in our old age.

Don't you worry, though, I'll only get someone in temporary. You'll find your old job waiting for you. You go, Megan my love. It'll be grand experience for you, and a different sort of life for a bit. I'll bet you might see your Owen from time to time, too. He tells me he's to take up his course again in October.'

'He's been talking to me, too, Dad, about himself.'

'Going to tell me, are you? Or would you rather not?'

Megan told him all she knew about Owen, and John Garreg listened.

When Megan had finished speaking, her father said, 'There's no chance he'll ever really find out any more details, you know. If he did come from this area there's no one left round here could prove it for him. He wants to stop looking for what he was, Megan, and to try and discover what he is, which is a lot more important. I think he's beginning to do it, too.'

When they were all ready for breakfast, Owen came in to say that Cariad's legs felt warm, and that though she could not be said to be lame, she walked a bit tenderly.

'It was all that rough going yesterday,' said Megan, contritely. 'I forget sometimes that she's not as young as she was.'

'I'd take her down to the sea, if I were you, young Owen. Let her cool her legs in the water. Seawater's a marvellous doctor for horses' legs.'

'Yes, you do that,' Megan said. 'I'll walk up with the dogs and see to the sheep on Long Way. You take Cariad down to the beach and you can look over the ones on the burrows as you go by.'

'Not before he's had his eggs and bacon he

won't,' said Mrs Garreg. 'Finish off what's in the pan, Owen. Megan's had hers.'

Megan went out, and Owen settled to his breakfast. 'It's good to see you eat like a Welshman at last,' Mrs Garreg said. 'No more appetite you had than a sick cat, when you first came.'

'I never met anyone before that can cook as well as you, Mrs Garreg,' Owen said, and she went quite pink with pleasure.

'You've made your mind up definite about going back to your studies in October have you?' John Garreg asked.

'Yes,' Owen said. 'That's what the college suggested. I'll be fine, by then. If I can stay here and work for you till October, it'll be as sure a cure as seawater for horses' legs!'

'Mind you,' John Garreg said, 'it'll be no rest cure. We don't twiddle our toes, you know, between one lambing season and the next, though some people seem to think so. We had some hikers come to the house one day last summer—called in for a drink of water. We don't get all that many coming by: most of the visitors stay down by the beach and don't venture this far up on the hill. They were country people, just like us, they said, from the south-east somewhere. They couldn't think how we spent our time, they said, with the sheep up there on the walks and us with no cattle to milk, no fences to mend, no crops to speak of. I really believe they thought it was the life of Riley.'

'"How sweet is the shepherd's sweet lot",' laughed Owen. 'What sort of farming were they in, then?'

'Oh, they weren't farmers. It turned out they

had a house on the edge of a village—one of those picture postcard ones: all black timbers and old red brick. The man went up to London each day to his business. Fancy travelling forty miles each morning before you can start work!'

'I don't fancy it at all,' Owen said.

'Well anyway, there were farms all round them, they said. Very modern. All the latest machinery, with all the livestock housed on concrete: chickens, pigs, veal calves. Ever so profitable, you can bet. If that was what they were used to, I suppose they probably thought we were being old-fashioned on purpose.'

'I won't, you can be sure of that,' Owen assured him. 'I'm looking forward to learning all that goes on in the year.'

'Look,' said John Garreg. 'I don't want to press you to anything you would not like, but when you're not at the university, when there's holidays and such, I'd be glad—we'd all be glad—if you'd spend any time you can spare here with us. That's true, isn't it Ma?'

'True as I stand here,' Eira Garreg said.

'Well, there's nothing I'd like better and that's for sure,' said Owen.

'Then I'll teach you more about sheep, and you can teach me more about your old rocks.'

'And you'll neither of you stop talking till the crack of doom I wouldn't wonder,' said Mrs Garreg. 'Make haste now. I've got that lad David to get off to school and I can hear the bus coming up the hill.'

When Owen went to join Megan, he found her wiping down one of the last of the expected lambs with a twist of soft hay. It had only just arrived in its new world, and its mother had had to struggle hard to deliver it. She would soon help with the drying of it but for a moment she lay exhausted, getting her strength.

'Poor old soul,' Megan said. 'She'd put a deal of effort into getting his head out, but then I found his legs were all in a twist and had to push him back to sort him out. Anyway it's a help to have small hands when there's that job to do.'

'Perhaps that's why they always have shepherdesses in the old nursery rhymes,' Owen said. 'On account of their little hands.'

'Oh,' said Megan, 'do you think I'd look good in a kirtled skirt and frilly pantaloons and a crook with ribbons on it?'

'Unbelievably,' said Owen, 'but not much use to the sheep!'

'Well, I'm off up the Long Way,' she said, 'the moment I've seen this fellow drinking well. You'll take Cariad down to the beach will you?'

'I'm just going to fetch her.'

They waved to each other as they set out in their opposite directions. Owen went down to the beach, with Cariad clattering beside him. Even Cariad could not manage the goats' descent from the top of the warren, so they would take the long track that skirted the village. Megan set out up the slope of the hill, with Mot and Glyn trotting at heel.

She took it slowly: it was a big area to cover on foot, and a steep climb to make at the start. There was a grey sky overhead, and though there was no rain in the wind, water still saturated the ground and the streams were still swollen, running fast and boisterous down the slopes. They had had no more casualties yet but Megan kept a sharp look-out for stock in trouble; listening for the bleat of a ewe separated from its lamb, or a youngster's pathetic wail when it could find no safe way across the tumbling water.

Higher and higher she climbed with the morning, until she came up onto the ride not far from the old bleak rocks of the Devil's Hat. From there she had a distant view of the beach where, ant-like in size, walked Owen up to his knees in the sea with Cariad sploshing along happily beside him. As Megan watched, he scrambled onto the pony's back, turned her head to the horizon and began to walk her further out into the sea. Megan could see, even from that distance, the change in her motion as she began to swim.

They headed out into deeper water, and a sudden fear took hold of Megan. Suppose they should just go on swimming? Suppose the old melancholy should overcome Owen and he should decide to swim and swim until the water went over his head, and he and Cariad were carried to the depths? She shook herself free of the thought, but was still relieved to see the two heads turn in an arc, and the swimming figures return to shore.

Close at hand the little Towy ran on down to the village, vigorous and full of water. From this point the village itself could not be seen, for it stood in a fold of land between the tops and the beach. She wondered what buzz of gossip was going round now about the sheep thieves, and how many people were murmuring that they'd always said Griffiths would come to no good, and that after all it was only what you'd expect from a family like that.

Megan was not a vengeful person, but she was glad they'd been caught and not just because of the loss of her father's sheep either. She would take a long time forgetting the terrible state of those ponies at Hafod. They were in good hands now, though. The policeman who had come to take statements had assured them of that.

She shivered suddenly. Cold, fat drops of rain fell on her neck, and she realized that heavier cloud had blown up round her while she had stood there looking at the landscape. She had not expected this turn of the weather. Normally she had an instinct for storm, as well as knowing the signs, well taught by her father, but there was no doubt she was about to be caught out now.

Already a mist of cloud was creeping between her and the sea, and Owen and the pony were no longer visible. She hoped they had turned safely for home.

Suddenly there was a fizzing in the air, and thunder cracked so unexpectedly overhead that Megan nearly fell. Glyn cowered miserably, and Mot began to pant with quick anxiety. Megan called them both to her and they began to look for a place to shelter before the storm should break all round them. They hid beneath a shelf of rock and watched the sky grow dark with the increasing thunder. Lightning licked and flickered across the blackness of cloud, and then crackled and fizzed to earth. The rain came so fast it was impossible to see beyond the rock's edge, but she could hear the roaring of the stream not far from where she huddled with the dogs.

She was not frightened: or at least, it was like no other kind of fear she felt—but her skin prickled when the lightning flashed, as if its electricity were inside herself. She wished it was over. They would not be too worried about her at home, for they knew she could take care of herself on the hill, but she felt they'd be glad to see her back again, for all that.

At last, when she felt so cramped and cold that it was an effort to move, the storm began to retreat, though still with its heavy artillery throwing the occasional defiance. She got up and crawled from her shelter with the dogs. She looked at the curled clouds above the Devil's Hat and as she did so there was, almost at the same time, a vicious crackle of lightning and the loudest thunder-clap she had ever heard. The little sapling that grew out of the rock split and flared like a match, and the great rock itself began to tilt and slide, slowly but unstoppably, from its perch on the rim of the hill.

Megan felt such horror at this that she could do nothing at all but stand and watch. The dogs pressed hard against her legs, unnerved by the storm's final outburst. She could feel their hearts thumping and the quickness of their breath, and her own blood sang in her ears. She could hear a noise, high and thin, beating in her head like a reedy bell: insistent and warning. She shook herself, but the noise continued, rousing her from her awful numbness just as the rock gathered speed and toppled from the edge to land athwart the little stream that raced downhill to join the Gwent. Soon, baulked by the rock, the water would search for a new way down and if it spilled to one side to join the Towy, there would be a great spate of water rushing down on Llanysaf in no time at all.

Megan began to run, the dogs bounding alongside, glad of some action to take their minds off their fear.

What with the noise of the wind in her ears and the fact that she had to keep a close watch on her footing over the rough hillside, she was aware of nothing but her own need to hurry. At the least the water could wash away the bridge and flood the houses on the banks. At worst there might be people drowned.

Suddenly she ran full-tilt into Owen and nearly knocked him down. She stared at him amazed.

'It's all right. It's all right,' he said. 'We know. You can stop running.'

She looked at him, quite unable to get enough breath to say anything, but desperate to warn him of the danger. If he could ride off on Cariad now, he might be in time.

He spoke firmly to her, as if she were demented, which indeed she almost was. Her horror of the rock had proved more than justified, and she had been running from nightmare, as well as bringing a warning.

'They're digging a channel to divert the water if it comes. They've got sandbags out. Do you understand? It's all right!'

At last she understood what he was saying, and slumped down on the grass, panting and almost sobbing.

'How did you know?' she said at last.

'I turned back from the beach when the storm began,' he said, 'but I hadn't gone all that far up the track when I felt there was something wrong.'

Megan looked sharply at him. Could he also have heard the bell? But there was no bell: not really. Just the beating of her own blood.

'I looked all round,' Owen went on, 'and there was nothing I could see that was amiss, so I went back down to the beach, in case there was anyone in trouble, though there had been no one about when I was there with Cariad. I spent a long time looking right out to sea, but there was nothing in sight: no people, no boats...' His voice trailed, and he looked hard at her for a moment, and she felt quite certain then that it was more than a vague unease that had warned him of the danger, though she doubted he would ever tell her. Perhaps he would always think it was his overtaxed mind playing tricks: a delusion of the brain.

'I turned round then, and looked up,' he said. 'There was mist on the hillside, but the Devil's Hat stood out clear above it and just as I looked there was that last great thundercrack and I could see that it was beginning to move. You were right after all. It must have been underpinned by soil that was washed away bit by bit with all the rain we've had, and when that little tree was hit, it toppled the whole thing over.'

'So you went down to warn the village?'

'No. I couldn't see from the beach just what would happen when the rock fell, but I knew you were up there somewhere, so we set off to fetch you, Cariad and me. I called out to tell some people as we came by Llanysaf though, and Old Tomas Prys said if by any chance the Devil had fallen across the stream they'd all be getting wetter than they bargained for before long, so I went with him to rouse up some of the men to help and then they packed me off here to find you.'

'Let's get back there now,' Megan said. 'We can give them a hand.'

Owen sat her up on Cariad and they set off down the hill. When they got to Llanysaf the stream was already beginning to roar with extra water, but the men had finished a channel above the village to let some of the spàte spill harmlessly down the hillside.

'Won't do more than drown a few rabbits,' Tomas Prys called out cheerfully. 'As well you dropped by, lad, or we'd all have wet feet by now.'

'I'll give them a hand with the sandbags,' Owen said, and he went off down the slope.

'You all right girl?' Tomas said. 'I hear you were up by the old Devil himself. It's as well he didn't fall on you now, isn't it?'

'I ran down to warn you, but Owen was here first,' she said. She paused and then added, 'When I was up there, I thought I heard a bell.'

'Bell?' he said. 'There's no bell by here girl.'

When they got back eventually to the farm, Eira Garreg would not rest until they were out of their wet things. They had hardly noticed, either of them, that they were soaked to the skin.

Only when they were dry and warm would she allow them to say one word about what had happened, or to tell John Garreg, who lay fuming with impatience to hear about the excitement of the day. The nurse had called in, and in between scolding him for doing too much she had given him a third-hand account of the storm and its results, but she only knew enough to assure the Garregs that Megan and Owen were quite safe.

When they sat down by the fire, with dry clothes on them and hot soup inside them, they were able at last to satisfy the shepherd's curiosity. He listened, quiet now and attentive, nodding with agreement when Megan said it was the worst storm she could ever remember;

smiling at Owen's reporting of some of Tomas Prys's funnier remarks.

Then Mrs Garreg called Owen to the scullery to bring in the coal and John Garreg reached out a hand to Megan when they were alone.

'Glad I am to see you safe, girl. You always hated that old rock, didn't you?'

'You're right,' Megan said.

'But they're all safe in the village? You're quite sure?'

'Quite sure, Dad. With Owen giving them a warning, they were well prepared.'

'Good,' said John Garreg quietly. 'That seems to put things right, somehow.'

'What did you say, Dad?' asked Megan.

'Nothing, love. Just thinking aloud,' her father replied.

After the storm, the evening cleared to sunshine. The sky was a bright, washed blue, and the low sun sparkled off the sea, making colours dance before the eyes. Owen and Megan sat on the short turf of the warren with the two dogs lying beside them. The air smelt of salt, and of the sweet bruised grass. Sheep grazed here and there: their fleeces turned golden-pink by the evening light and overhead, the gulls, who had come wheeling back from their sheltered places when the storm was spent, soared and swooped above them and planed on scimitar wings down to the sea.

## *About the Author*

Anne Knowles now runs a small farm in Gloucestershire where she has a handful of sheep, two pigs, a calf, some hens and 'more ponies than I can afford'. She first became interested in sheep when she rescued one ewe thrown out of the flock because she was knock-kneed and kept falling over. She named her Uriah Sheep—because her disability gave her such a humble aspect!